Joseph Stratford

Wiltshire and its worthies

notes topographical and biographical

Joseph Stratford

Wiltshire and its worthies
notes topographical and biographical

ISBN/EAN: 9783337373924

Printed in Europe, USA, Canada, Australia, Japan

Cover: Foto ©ninafisch / pixelio.de

More available books at **www.hansebooks.com**

WILTSHIRE AND ITS WORTHIES:

NOTES

TOPOGRAPHICAL AND BIOGRAPHICAL.

BY

JOSEPH STRATFORD,

AUTHOR OF "GOOD AND GREAT MEN OF GLOUCESTERSHIRE," &c. &c.

" There is an eager desire, of which all mankind, perhaps, are sensible, to attain some tangible or visible memorial of the great men of other days ; to visit the spots they frequented, to linger in the ruins of their habitations, the scenes in which their great deeds were performed, the tombs in which their ashes repose."

G. POULETT SCROPE,

At Inaugural Meeting of the Wilts Archæological and Natural History Society, 1853.

𝔖𝔞𝔩𝔦𝔰𝔟𝔲𝔯𝔶 :
BROWN AND CO.
LONDON: SIMPKIN, MARSHALL & CO.

1882.

THIS VOLUME

PREFACE.

A WILTSHIRE author has pithily said that a short book should no more have a long preface than a small house a large portico. According to this rule mine ought to be brief.

The present volume had its origin in a series of sixteen papers which appeared in *The Wilts and Gloucestershire Standard*, in the spring and summer of 1881. They were introduced by the following remarks :—

" It may seem an impertinence for one who is neither a native nor a resident of the county, to offer " *Notes on Wiltshire and its Worthies.*" Generous minds will find explanation and excuse in the following facts.

" My father was a Wiltshire man. My paternal grandfather sleeps under the shadow of St. Sampson's noble tower at Cricklade, a photograph of which is daily before my eyes. Other ancestors and relatives rest in the churchyards of Blunsdon, Lattou, Eisey, and neighbouring parishes. Wiltshire traditions, including the two-fold version of the moonraking legend, were "household words" in my early home ; and Stonehenge was a favourite family picture. Visits to Wiltshire were among the pleasures of my youth. Many of my most intimate friends of later life have been Wiltshire men. For twenty-seven years I resided near the north-western end of the shire, often visiting some of its towns and villages, and having much intercourse with its people.

" More than a quarter of a century ago, I read to a Young Men's Society a paper on some of the Poets whose names are inseparably associated with this county. Subsequently I began to collect notes of its Worthies in general. These I intended to weave into a popular lecture, to be given at Cricklade, and at the delivery of which I had reason to think my late friend, the much respected Richard Mullings, Esq., of Cirencester, a native of Bishop's Cannings, and Town Clerk of Cricklade, would have presided. Circumstances prevented my carrying this design into effect, and for a time my work was stayed. 1880, the centenary of my father's birth, recalled my attention to the subject ; and the results will be presented in the series of papers of which this is the first."

In compiling these papers I was often embarrassed by the abundance of materials; and my difficulty was to select and condense. Correspondence and further researches added to the stock, the possession of which suggested an extension of the work and its re-issue in a more permanent form. This course was also urged by friends in Wiltshire and elsewhere.

In making these extensions I have received kind and valuable help from W. C. Kemm, Esq., of Amesbury. This gentleman has not only forwarded me a large quantity of interesting topographical and biographical materials, but also furnished some such excellently written sketches that I have given them with as little alteration as my plan would allow. It was also in the heart of another gentleman of Amesbury, Job Edwards, Esq., to have afforded me kindly aid, had not illness unfortunately prevented his doing so.

My thanks for the use of valuable books are due to W. R. Brown, Esq., of Trowbridge, John Mullings, Esq., of Cirencester ; and many others.

Some further obligations are acknowledged in the body of the work.

J. S.

GLOUCESTER,
September, 1882.

INDEX OF PERSONS.

INDEX OF PLACES.

WILTSHIRE AND ITS WORTHIES.

INTRODUCTION.

"Wiltshire is a fine, a remarkable, a truly interesting county." JOHN BRITTON.

"Without wishing to draw any invidious comparisons between this county and other parts of England, I may say I scarcely know any district so rich as ours—it is a perfect epitome of history." LORD SIDNEY HERBERT.

E are now in an upper northern part of the county of Wilts. If we could take our stand on some Pisgah, and looking southward, view the land as it lies before us, we should see that it spreads out in a rather elliptical shape, but somewhat round at its north head, and somewhat square at its south base. Its extreme length from north to south is fifty-seven miles; its greatest breadth from east to west is thirty-four miles. On the north, it is bounded by Gloucestershire; on the east, by Berkshire and Hampshire; on the south, by Hampshire and Dorsetshire; and on the west, by Somersetshire and Gloucestershire. Within its area there are about 870,000 acres, of which nearly 800,000 are arable, meadow, or pasture land. The population, which in 1801 was 185,107, had increased in 1871 to 257,177; consisting of 126,828 males and 130,849 females. The census of 1881 shows a small increase, the total population amounting to 258,967.

The surface of the country presents a variety of features. The north part, including a portion of the White Horse Vale, consists mainly of rich arable and pasture lowlands, with gentle risings here and there. It is well watered by many fine streams, and is famous for its excellent dairy produce. Across the middle of the shire, from Savernake Forest on the east by the Black Heath to Westbury on the west, runs an irregular range of hills. Marlborough Downs are on the north side; and on the south side stretch those extensive downs which form the famous Salisbury Plain. In the south-east portion of the county there are wide-spreading ranges of chalk hills, covered with good soil and in a high state of cultivation. Here, as well as in the north and among the mid-shire downs, there are scenes of much picturesqueness and beauty.

The Bristol Avon, the Salisbury Avon, the Nadder, the Wiley, and some smaller rivers, rise in Wiltshire or flow through it. None of these streams are of much use for navigation, but they contribute greatly to the beauty and fertility of the districts through which they pass.

There are several lines of canal in the north, but the south is almost without this accommodation. Various railway systems intersect the county in different parts. Looking at a Geological map, it will be seen that while the north and north-west parts of Wilts belong to the Oolite formations, the north-east and south portions belong to the chalk. "Its geological formation," says Mr. Scrope, "is of a very simple character. It contains no older rocks than the upper beds of the Lias, nor any newer than the chalk, except a few patches of clay and gravel belonging to the Eocene Tertiaries upon the surface of its chalk downs, and the alluvial beds of its existing river valleys. Moreover, these strata appear to have suffered comparatively little disturbance; the whole series lying 'conformably,' that is, in parallel beds, one over the other. On the other hand, within this limited range the structure of our county exhibits a most instructive and interesting variety of sedimentary and fossiliferous strata, well displayed and easily studied."

Ecclesiastically this county is in the province of Canterbury; and chiefly in the diocese of Salisbury; the deaneries of Cricklade and Malmesbury, comprising about 80 parishes and districts, and also the parish of Marston Maisey, being in that of Gloucester and Bristol.

Its parliamentary divisions are North and South; and are in pretty equal proportion, the dividing line being drawn from Chilton on the east to Westbury on the west. Each contains seventeen hundreds.

It was a quaint conceit of John Aubrey, that there was a marked difference between the people of the north and the south. This difference as described by him was by no means flattering to that part of the county to which he himself belonged. Speaking of the north and its inhabitants, he says :—"It is a woodsere country, abounding with sour and austere plants, as sorrel, &c., which makes their humours sour : *Mem*. North Wiltshire is very worm-woodish, and more litigious than South Wilts." One would imagine that the old antiquarian was himself under the influence of these "sour plants" when he wrote this uncomplimentary *Mem*.

Of the peculiar excellencies of any particular portion of the inhabitants, or of the merits of the people of the county in general, we do not now treat. It will be our aim to single out those who in past times became men of note ; and to record their names in association with the places to which they belonged.

The number of men who rise to eminence and obtain names which pass down to posterity is comparatively small. Genius is rare ; distinguished abilities belong to few ; and great deeds are only occasionally achieved. Thousands of lives do not rise to mediocrity ; and even when this is reached and passed, celebrity is not necessarily gained. Serviceable talents may be exercised and useful lives spent without securing present special attention or future fame. When therefore we meet with names shining in the records of human history—whether in the annals of a kingdom or a parish —it is interesting to note their existence and mark the causes which render them conspicuous.

Biography serves important uses. Ages before Longfellow sang—

> "Lives of great men all remind us
> We may make our lives sublime ;"

or even Plutarch had penned his lives of glorious Greeks, minds and hearts had been stirred and purified by the records of noble deeds and moral excellence. A good life is, in a sense, perpetuated by memorials of its works, and a worthy character continues to shine in the delineation of its virtues. The original may perish and pass from sight, but faithful portraits will preserve its memory and extend its influence. It is the work of the biographer to perpetuate, for the good of future generations, that which has proved beneficial to the past.

Genius and worth are the heritage of the world. The gifted and the excellent belong not to one age or one land alone, but to the whole race through all time. Human hearts in every land awed by the pencil of Raphael or thrilled by the music of Handel feel kinship with these gifted spirits, and appropriate them as the common property of the race. Nevertheless there is an important sense in which the illustrious one belongs to the nation of his birth; and may be specially claimed by the spot where his life began or his years were spent.

The honour of such special proprietorship has ever been highly esteemed. Did not seven cities claim to have been the birthplace of Homer? and does not the little Avon-side town of Stratford lift its head high among the renowned spots of the world, as the cradle and grave of Shakespeare? Many a mighty city, rich and influential in itself, yet feels that it adds to its glory by the erection of a memorial to some illustrious citizen.

Localities become more interesting when written over with history's pen; and even natural scenes acquire fresh charms from being linked with noble names and worthy deeds. In words eloquent as Carlyle's own, one of his biographers has said :—

"How the charm would be lessened that we find in the scenery of our native land, how much less potent would be the influence of that scenery in the formation of character, were it not for such associations as these? Without the moral influence derived from humanity, the physical beauty and grandeur would count for comparatively little; even the most splendid prospects in nature assert but a limited power over the mind until they have been linked to the story of noble lives. What are the fields, however good for growing corn, that have been hallowed by no memories of martyr and hero? the rivers that are songless but for their own natural music? the mountains that are no more associated with human life than are the clouds which mantle round their summits? Not merely for their natural loveliness do we visit those lakes on whose woody shores dwelt Southey and Coleridge, De Quincey and Arnold, Wilson and Wordsworth. Sheffield, with its clang of hammers, and thick smoke curtain, looks less grim when we think of Ebenezer Elliott and James Montgomery. Byron and Kirke White deepen the romance of Sherwood Forest, and send a pathos through Wilford Grove ; the whole of woody Warwickshire becomes like a fairyland at the thought of Shakespeare ; even the dull banks of the sleepy Ouse are glorified by the Farmer of St. Ives and the Bedford Tinker—the one the doer of the greatest deeds, the other the dreamer of the grandest dream, that fill with so much meaning the name of England."

Local biography may, therefore, be thought to possess peculiar interest : and the inhabitants of particular places may be expected to welcome records of the great and the good who have been connected with the same spots in years gone by. The County of Wilts has not been unfruitful in eminent men ; and the Worthies of Wiltshire might supply biographical materials for a goodly volume. Brief notes, gathered from a variety of sources, will be all that will be attempted here. We shall meet with names of which not only Wiltshire but all England is justly proud ; we shall also meet with others comparatively little known ; and, perhaps, with some which may be deemed notorious rather than famous, but of which we shall make passing mention.

A few words as to the plan of this work. A line running from Jarvis' Quarry, in the parish of Kemble, in the north, to Tollard Royal in the south ; and another from Hannington in the north through Odstock in the south, would divide the county into three longitudinal strips of about eleven miles each in breadth. These strips will be called West Wilts, Mid Wilts, and East Wilts respectively. The Parliamentary division line crossing the shire from Chilton to Westbury bisects these strips, and gives us three northern and three southern parts : these will be—

WEST WILTS—*North* and *South*.
MID WILTS —*North* and *South*.
EAST WILTS—*North* and *South*.

In following the course I have marked out, we shall travel down the western side of the county, and then bending eastward reach its capital city. Thence we shall return northward in a devious line through the middle of the shire to the upper end, from which, turning our faces to the south-east, we shall pass along the eastern side till we again come to Salisbury. Here, pausing, we shall, in conclusion, notice a variety of interesting facts relating particularly to the social and religious history of the county.

In pursuing our way we shall be often tempted to pause. Pleasant hills will invite us to climb their slopes, and gentle streams to wander along their banks. We shall pass many an ancient church and many a noble mansion where we might well linger in interested and admiring contemplation ; while we shall find it hard not to tarry amidst those wondrous monuments of antiquity for which the Downs of Marlborough and the Plain of Salisbury are so justly famed. Almost contemporaneously with the first publication of these Notes a leading daily Journal, referring to Stonehenge and " the unequalled series of earth and stone monuments which lie to the north of it," remarked—" There are few curiosities, as they used to be called, in England better worth visiting, none perhaps more impressive in themselves and fuller of suggestion (when the neighbouring Old Sarum and Clarendon, Salisbury Cathedral and Wilton, the battlefields of the seventeenth century, and the rotten boroughs of the eighteenth are taken with it) in historical memories. In these holidays any one who is original enough to take a not particularly celebrated English county as his playground may try Wiltshire, provided he does not set his heart upon mountains and waterfalls, or gambling tables and loose company, or unpleasant tasting waters, or Scotch hotel bills, with a very excellent chance of satisfaction." But these pleasant tasks must be left for those who have more leisure ; and our one aim already indicated must be steadily kept in view.

In our travels we shall ask information from gossiping John Aubrey, and from his more careful and accurate fellow county man John Britton. The topographer Cooke, and the county historian Sir Richard Hoare, will afford us help. Items of biography will be gathered from quaint Thomas Fuller, Professor Henry Morley, and numerous other sources. Especially shall we derive assistance from the invaluable writings of one to whom Wiltshire owes a deep debt of gratitude, as a most diligent and successful student and expositor of its history and antiquities—the Rev. John Edward

Jackson, M.A., F.S.A., Rector of Leigh Delamere and Hon. Canon of Bristol. As Editor of Aubrey's "Collections," as one of the Secretaries of the Wilts Archæological and Natural History Society, joint Editor of its admirable Magazine and frequent contributor to its pages, the labours of this gentleman have largely increased and enriched the literature of the county. Many and worthy, too, have been his co-workers; and from some of these we shall gain many an interesting fact as we go on our way. In not a few instances we shall be indebted to the courtesy of various correspondents, both in Wiltshire and elsewhere, for information which could not be obtained from other quarters. The aid of that venerable and willing, but not always reliable authority—"An old inhabitant"—will also be occasionally rendered.

PART I.

WEST WILTS.—*NORTH.*

"Methinkes it shewes a kind of gratitude and good nature to revise the memories and memorials of the pious and charitable Benefactors since dead and gone."

Jo. Awdrey.

"It is in every man's power to do a very great deal of good. This is the main thing, that every one of us should individually exert himself to do his best."

Right Hon. T. H. S. Sotheron Estcourt.

THE most northerly parish of the county on its western side is that of *Kemble.* This once secluded rural village was the birth-place of

HENRY HATCHER,

who was born May 14th, 1777. He was the son of a small farmer; and his education was commenced at a school in Cirencester. It was continued at Salisbury whither his parents removed; and at fourteen he became junior assistant in the school where he had been placed. After filling similar situations in other schools, he became at the age of eighteen, amanuensis to the Rev. William Coxe, of Bemerton. From this time his literary and archæological labours in connection with Mr. Coxe, Sir R. C. Hoare, and Mr. Benson, as well as his own independent efforts, were unceasing. In a letter to John Britton, dated January, 1848, he thus refers to the works and pursuits of his past life :—"Last year was the fiftieth since I became in some degree connected with literature. In that interval twenty-five quarto volumes have passed through my hands as amanuensis or editor. I have written one quarto, two octavos, and a folio of about 800 pages. I have acquired twelve languages or dialects, and I have dabbled with many other matters of which I am scarcely suspected. Through all this I have waded ; I may safely say by my own exertions ;

and I have still at sixty-five, to work hard for a livelihood. Our dear and valued country is a precious place for those who do not understand the direct art of money-getting. I sometimes fancy it cannot be so everywhere." To this he might have added that for many years he had the toil and responsibility of a school which he commenced and successfully conducted in Salisbury. His death occurred suddenly December 14th, 1847. The Dean and Chapter and other inhabitants of Salisbury erected a tablet to his memory in the Cathedral; and his friend Britton wrote his Memoirs.

The extreme north point of Kemble parish is *Jarvis Quarry*, just two miles south-west of Cirencester, on the ancient Acman Street. From this point the boundary line of the shire runs on the east side of the Roman way, so that the traveller does not enter Wiltshire till Jackament's Bottom is passed, when the line crosses the old road and keeps on its west side to the parish of *Ashley*. A mile or so brings us to *Long Newnton*, south and west of which runs the infant Avon, separating this Wiltshire parish from the Gloucestershire one of Shipton Moyne, where Estcourt Park surrounding Estcourt House, abuts upon this dividing stream. With these parishes the name of the Right Honourable

THOMAS HENRY SUTTON SOTHERON ESTCOURT,

is inseparably associated. By residence and property in these border parishes he belonged to both counties: Gloucestershire claims him as a member of one of its oldest families; Wiltshire claims him as one of its truest friends. He was the son of Thomas Grimston Estcourt, of the ancient family of Estcourt, which has been settled in Gloucestershire, and held property at Shipton Moyne, for nearly 600 years. His mother was Eleanor, daughter and co-heiress of James Sutton, of New Park, Devizes. He was their eldest son, and was born in London on April 4th, 1801, and christened at St. George's, Hanover Square, May 15th. After being at Harrow, he went to Oriel College, Oxford; taking his M.A. degree in 1826. In 1829 he entered Parliament as member for Marlborough; and the following year married Lucy Sarah, daughter of Admiral Frank Sotheron, of Kirklington, Notts, whose name he assumed by sign manual in 1839; re-assuming his paternal name by the same process in 1855.

He was member for Devizes from 1835 to 1844, when he succeeded Sir Francis Burdett as one of the representatives of North Wilts—a position he continued to hold till the state of his health obliged him to retire from public affairs in 1874. As a supporter of Lord Derby's Administration his abilities were recognised by the Premier, by whom he was appointed President of the Poor Law Board in 1858; and successor of Mr. Walpole in the Home Office the following year. While diligently and effectively discharging parliamentary and official duties, he was ever mindful of the interests of his constituents, and alive to the promotion of local improvements. As a pleasant illustration of the way in which he 'magnified his office' as representative of the Northern division of the county, it is related that on one occasion at a public dinner, where some little discussion of North and South interests occurred, he said playfully, in answer to some argument of Sidney Herbert—"Yes; you represent the *chalk*, and I the *cheese*."

Among the many philanthropic works of his actively useful life, that connected with the Wilts Friendly Society deserves especial mention. This institution, intended for the benefit of the working classes, was established in 1828; "but," says a writer in the *Devizes Gazette*, "little came of it till Mr. Estcourt took it in hand. He put his whole heart and soul into it. Day after day, for weeks together, he would attend meetings, and walk to church in processions, followed at first by few, and exciting laughter, but afterwards attended by a goodly gathering. He thought no trouble too great, if he could establish what he believed to be one great means of raising not merely the material, but also the moral tone of the working classes in Wiltshire." His efforts were not in vain. This Society has spread its ramifications not only to nearly all parts of Wilts, but to many parishes in East Gloucestershire also. At its Jubilee, which was celebrated in 1879, it numbered 9,816 benefit and 1,003 honorary members; it contained 115 branches; and its total funds amounted to no less a sum than £36,618. Mr. Estcourt greatly rejoiced in its success; and it will probably prove "an enduring monument to his fame."

The many excellencies of his private character as well as the usefulness of his public works contributed to his great popularity. Generous and genial, a Christian gentleman, cheerfully and gracefully fulfilling the duties of daily life, he possessed the esteem of those who knew him in private as well as the respect of those who saw only his public career. "I think," says his friend Earl Nelson, "I may say that he was full of love and of kindness in all the relations of life. Those who knew him in his own home are aware that he was looked up to by his labourers, and those who who were round about him as a very father." Nor was his kindness limited to man. A gentleman who never saw him but once says: "His conduct on that occasion, in reference to a suffering animal, gave me a most favourable impression of his character."

He died January 6, 1876, and was buried, according to his own wish, in a private and simple manner at Shipton Moyne Church. In this hallowed place, where he had so long been accustomed to worship, and which he loved so well, his family have since erected a handsome stained window to his memory. The subjects illustrated are from the life of St. John the Baptist: one, the angel announcing the future birth of St. John to Zacharias; the other, St. John in the dungeon about to be taken to execution. Each subject occupies two compartments of a five light West window.

A noble Fountain surmounted by a Statue, erected in the Market Place, Devizes, was unveiled amidst great demonstrations of honour, September 16th, 1879. It cost about £1,500, and bears the following inscription :—

"Erected MDCCCLXXIX., by public subscription, to the memory of the Right Hon. Thomas H. S. Sotheron Estcourt, Member of Parliament for Marlborough, Devizes, and North Wilts, for the period of XXXIII years. Founder of the Wilts Friendly Society.

Charlton, a few miles to the east, as we pass from Newnton to Malmesbury, reminds us of the Howards. At the dissolution of Abbeys this manor was purchased by Mr. William Stumpe, of Malmesbury, whose son, Sir James Stumpe, became Sheriff of Wilts in 1551. Sir James married Bridget, daughter of Sir Edward Baynton, of Bromham. Their daughter, Isabel, became the wife of a Cornish knight, Sir Henry Knyvett, and died in 1585. Sir Henry, who, Aubrey says, had some command in Queen Elizabeth's forces at the time of the Spanish Armada, died in 1598. A monument, with effigies of himself and wife, still stands in Charlton

Church. Their eldest daughter, Katharine, became the second wife of Lord Thomas Howard, son of the Duke of Norfolk, who thus obtained the manor. He was a distinguished naval officer, and was created Earl of Suffolk in 1603. His second son, some years after, was raised to the peerage as Earl of Berkshire. The latter resided at Charlton, and his son,

SIR ROBERT HOWARD,

born 1626, figured among the literary men of the reign of Charles II. Possessing literary tastes and some poetical ability he wrote songs and sonnets, and several dramatic pieces. An intimate friendship was formed between him and Dryden, who in the autumn of 1663 was assisting him in the composition of his play of *The Indian Queen*. In prosecution of this work Dryden came with his friend to Earl Berkshire's at Charlton. Play writing was varied by wooing, and John Dryden, the poet, won the Earl's daughter, Lady Elizabeth Howard, for wife. The courtship was short; they were married in December. The drama was also completed; *The Indian Queen*, all written in heroic couplets, appearing the following month.

On the breaking out of the plague, Dryden left London, and came to the house of his father-in-law, where he and Sir Robert continued to indulge their literary tastes, especially discussing the merits of rhyme and blank verse. Dryden's eldest son was born at Charlton in 1665 or 1666, during which years the poet remained there. His poem, *Annus Mirabilis*, the wonderful year, in which he celebrated the Fire of London, and a great sea fight with the Dutch, was written during this long visit; as was also a reply to his brother-in-law Sir Robert, in discussion on blank verse. This latter production appeared in his *Essays of Dramatic Poesy*.

It was in a ploughed field near Charlton pond, that Major Whyte-Melville met an untimely end by a fall from his horse, while hunting with the Vale of White Horse hounds. As the author of numerous popular works of fiction, Major Whyte-Melville was widely known; and as a gentleman of genial and benevolent character was highly esteemed by a large circle of friends. He died at the age of 59.

Just south of Charlton is *Garsdon*. Of this Manor Aubrey makes the

13

following "*Mem:* That one Mody was a footeman to King Henry the Eighth, who falling from his horse as he was hawkeing, I think on Harneslow Heath, fell with his head into mudde, with which being fatt and heavy, he had been suffocated to death, had he not been timely relieved by his footman Mody: for which service after the dissolution of the Abbies, he gave him the Manour of Garsden."

Other notes pertaining to this parish have a special interest for our American cousins, particularly those—and they are not few—who are of Wiltshire descent. The chancel of the little church, which is pleasantly situated on an eminence, contains a monumental slab to the memory of Sir Lawrence Washington, who was second son in the Northamptonshire family, from the elder branch of which General Washington descended. Sir Lawrence purchased Garsden from the Moodys. The inscription on the stone runs thus :—"Sir Lawrence Washington, Kt., lately Chief Register of the Chancery, whom it pleased God to take unto his peace from the fury of the insuing wars. Oxon, May 4 : here interred 24th A.D. 1643, aged 64. Also Dame Ann his wife died June 13 : buried 16th 1645.

> "Hic patrios cineres curavit filius urna
> Condere qui tumulo nunc jacet ille pius."

The Church plate consisting of a flagon, two chalices, and a salver, all of silver, is engraved—"Given to Garsden Church by the Lady Pargiter, formerly wife of Sir Lawrence Washington, who both lie buried here."

A little more than two miles brings us to *Malmesbury,* anciently a town of much importance. Beautiful for situation, defended by strong fortifications, and adorned with a fine abbey, it ranked among the chief places of this part of the kingdom. The monastery owed its foundation to Maildulph, or Meldrum as he is sometimes called, an Irish or Scotch monk, who came from his own country and pitched his tent or built his cell at Malmesbury, in the seventh century. The abbey, which Leland calls "a right magnificent thing," was built by

ALDHELM,

who, under the head of "Saints," ranks first among Fuller's *Wiltshire Worthies.* Aldhelm, said by some to be the son of a weaver, by others to have been " well born and well taught," joined the poor monastery in 672. He was then a youth of sixteen, but soon became the founder's chief disciple, and was elected his successor at his death. His energies and his possessions were freely devoted to the interests of the institution; and at length he undertook the erection of the abbey. In the accomplishment of this great work he was assisted by the Bishop of Winchester; and as it progressed he was encouraged by grants from kings and nobles for its support. He was held in high repute, and his influence both with monks and people was great and good. He inspired in his religious companions a zeal for a pure life, and laboured in various ways to bring the inhabitants of the district under religious influence and instruction. It is said he was both a poet and a musician, playing all the instruments of music used at that time. " He was the first of the English nation," says Aubrey, " that wrote Latin, and that taught the Englishmen the way how to make a Latin verse. He was canonised a saint, and on his Festival Day (March 31) there was kept here a great faire," which was held in a meadow called St. Aldhelm's mead. His writings included two treatises—*De Virginitate* and *Ænigmata*; he is also said to have translated the Psalms of David into the vernacular tongue. Fuller, while giving him high praise, yet adds, " Impudent monks have much abused his memory with *shameless lyes*, and amongst the rest with a *wooden miracle*, that a carpenter having cut a *beam* for his church too *short*, he by his prayers stretched it out to its full proportion. To this I may add another *lye* as clear as the *sun* itself, on whose *rayes* (they report) he hung his *vestment*, which miraculously supported it to the great admiration of the beholders."

He went to Rome to be consecrated Bishop of Sherborne, and returning home lived in great esteem till his death in 709. This event occurred under circumstances worth recording. He was engaged in his episcopal work at Doulting, a small village near Shepton Mallet, when he felt himself smitten for death. He straightway directed his attendants to carry him into the little wooden church, when commending his soul to God he tranquilly breathed his last. The church at Doulton is dedicated to him. He was buried at Malmesbury, and his shrine was long held in high veneration.

In the tenth century a great benefactor to Malmesbury appeared in

KING ATHELSTAN,

the favourite grandson of Alfred the Great. Its inhabitants, by the aid they rendered him in some battle with the Danes about the year 930, found special favour in his eyes, and received from him a substantial proof of this in his gift of the Royal Heath. This tract of 500 acres of land was given to "the burgesses of Malmesbury and their successors for ever." It was enclosed in 1821, and is now held in shares according to some established rules. No wonder that "the memory of Athelstan is a household word at Malmesbury." The monastery also received large gifts at his hands. Here he buried two of his nephews who fell in the great fight with the Danes; and here, most likely according to his own wish, he himself was laid to rest, after dying at Gloucester in 941.

OLIVER OF MALMESBURY

is described as a great mathematician and mechanic. Fuller says he was also addicted to astrology, and wrote some books on that art. Little, however, is known concerning either his acquirements or his works; but a curious account is given of his death. In the exercise of his mechanical ingenuity, he made wings for his hands and feet, and imagined that with these he could fly. Resolving to make the experiment, he ascended a tower in the town, and attempted to take his flight. It was not altogether a failure; but after having fluttered about a furlong, he fell heavily to the ground, breaking both his thighs, so that he shortly afterwards died, in the year 1060.

WILLIAM OF MALMESBURY

was a native of Somersetshire; "but," says Fuller, "quitting his own name of Summerset, he assumed that of Malmesbury, because there he had (if not born) his best preferment." He was but a boy when early in the thirteenth century he entered the Monastery. Love of learning probably influenced him in taking this step, as much as religious feeling. Books became his companions and he actively engaged in literary work; preferring the office of librarian to that of abbot. His chief work, "The History of the Kings of England," was dedicated to Robert, Earl of Gloucester, a man of taste and a patron of learning. Fuller praises this production as "an History to be honoured, both for the truth and method thereof;" and with his usual quaintness thus excuses its weak points :—"If any fustiness be found in his writings, it comes not from the grape, but from the cask. The smack of superstition in his books is not to be imputed to his person, but to the age wherein he lived." More recent critics have also estimated him highly as a writer "who almost rose from the chronicler into the historian." It is thought that he died in 1142, at the age of 47.

We may here mention another member of the Abbey fraternity—William of Colerne, who was Abbot the latter part of the thirteenth century. Of his learning, his religious zeal, or his good works we know nothing, but Canon Jackson tells us "he was famous for improving the creature comforts of the monks," and that in a Register of the Abbey "he is stated to have planted vineyards, laid out gardens, made fishponds, and when he made an Anniversary for himself, his father and mother, he directed that with the money a cask of the best wine should also be bought, and first tasted on that day." He died in 1296.

Aubrey, who was the friend and biographer of

THOMAS HOBBES,

the philosopher, tells us that he was the son of an ignorant parish priest of Westport, Malmesbury, where he was born in a humble cottage, at the corner of the Horse Fair, April 5, 1588. A quarrel, leading to an assault on another parson at the Church door, obliged the Vicar of Westport to seek safety in flight. His elder brother, a wealthy glover in the town, seems to have provided for the education of his young nephew when he was thus left as it were fatherless. The boy received instruction in a private school from Mr. Robert Latymer, then or afterwards rector of Leigh Delamere. At the age of fifteen he entered Magdalen Hall, Oxford. On leaving college he accompanied the son of Lord Hardwicke through France and Italy, and on his return became secretary to Lord Hardwicke himself. About this time he formed friendships with Lord Bacon and Ben Jonson, translating some of the works of the former into Latin, and having one of his own productions revised by the latter. Lord Bacon, who engaged him as his secretary, entertained a high opinion of his abilities. His pupil, who became Earl of Devonshire, died early, and Hobbes was appointed tutor to his son, the young Earl, then thirteen years of age. He took him, as he had taken his father, to travel on the continent, after which they returned to Chatsworth—the seat of the Devonshire family. Here Hobbes wrote a poem in Latin on the wonders of the Peak, " *De Mirabilibus Pecci.* " In 1641, " smelling the battle afar off," and apprehensive of troubles in the coming struggle between the King and Parliament, he retired to France, and there began those works on which his fame as a moral and political philosopher is based. The chief of these bore the title of " *Leviathan; or the Matter, Form, and Power of a Commonwealth, Ecclesiastical and Civil;* " and was not published till 1651. Returning to England he resided at Chatsworth, where his literary work was industriously carried on ; politics, mathematics, religion, and poetry occupying his powerful brain and his busy pen. A Latin poem on his own Life was written at the age of eighty-four ; and his death did not occur till 1679, when he was ninety-two.

Few writers have met with more opposition than the Philosopher of Malmesbury. The supposed atheistic tendency of his opinions called forth strong condemnation, and he was freely denounced as an infidel of the worst stamp. We cannot here enter into this matter. Suffice it to say that some who appear to best understand his writings and character think this accusation unjust. At the same time it cannot be denied that the influence of his works has been to a great extent unfavourable to some forms of Christianity. Professor Henry Morley remarks, " No man can hurt religion by being as true as it is in his power to be—and that Hobbes was;" and adds, in a spirit of large charity, " Our judgment of a man ought never to depend upon whether or not we agree with him in opinion."

"Hobbes," says another writer," was honest, kind, moderate, communicative and of unrelaxing application." His habits were singular. " At Chatsworth he gave his mornings to exercise and paying his respects to the family and its visitors ; at noon he went to his study, ate his dinner alone without ceremony, shut himself in with ten or twelve pipes of tobacco and gave his mind free play." Aubrey gives us a glimpse of his person. "This summer 1634 (I remember it was the venison season, July or August) Mr. Thomas Hobbes came into his native country to visit his friends, and amongst others he came to see his old Schoolmaster, Mr. Latimer, at Leigh Delamere, when I was then a little youth at school in the church, newly entered into my grammar by him. Here was the first place and time that I ever had the honour to see this worthy learned man, who was then pleased to take notice of me, and the next day came and visited my relations. He was a proper man, briske, and in very good equipage; his hair was then quite black."

Two or three members of the Stumpe or Stumps family, of Malmesbury, are deemed worthy of notice by Fuller. Of

T. STUMPS

whom he describes as "one of the most eminent clothiers in England," he tells the following story :—" King Henry the Eighth, hunting one day in Bredon Forest, came with all his court train, unexpectedly to dine with the clothier. But great housekeepers are as seldom surprised with guests as a vigilant Captain with enemies. Stumps commands his little army of workmen, which he fed daily in his house, to fast one meal until night (which they might easily do without endangering their health), and with the same provision gave the King and his court train (though not so delicious and various) yet wholesome and plentiful entertainment."

His reference to

WILLIAM STUMPS,

who bought the Abbey and its demeans from Henry the Eighth for "fifteen pounds, two shillings, and a half-penny," closes with a witty wish for " more *Branches* from such *Stumps*, who by their bounty may preserve the monuments of antiquity from destruction."

Aubrey, thinking, " 'Tis pity the strange adventures of

CAPTAIN THOMAS STUMP,

of Malmesbury, should be forgotten," proceeds to relate the following extraordinary account :—"He was the oldest sonn of Mr. Will. Stump, rector of Yatton Keynell; was a boy of a most daring spirit; he would climb towers and trees most dangerously; nay, he would walk on the battlements of the tower there. He had too much spirit to be a scholar, and about sixteen went in a voyage with his uncle, since Sir Thomas Ivy, to Guyana, in anno 1633 or 1632. When the ship put in some where there, four of five of them straggled into the countrey too far, and in the interim the winds served, and the sails were hoist, and the stragglers left behind. It was not long before the wild people seized on them and stript them, and those that had beards they knocked their braines out, and (as I remember) did eat them; but the Queen saved T. Stump, and the other boy. Stump threw himself into the river Oronoque to have drowned himself, but could not sinke; he is very full chested. The other youth shortly died. He lived with them till 1636 or 1637. His narrations are very strange and pleasant; but so many years since have made me almost forget all. He says there is incomparable fruite there, and that it may be termed the paradise of the world. He says that the spondyles of the backbones of the huge serpents there are used to sit on, as our women sit upon butts. He taught them to build hovills, and to thatch and wattle. I wish I had a good account of his abode there : he is *fide dignus*. I never heard of any man that lived so long among those salvages. A ship then sayling by, a Portughese, he swam to it; and they took him up and made use of him for a seaboy. As he was sayling near Cornwall he stole out of a porthole, and swam to shore ; and so begged to his father's in Wiltshire. When he came home, nobody knew him, and they would not own him; only Jo. Harris the carpenter knew him. At last he recounted so many circumstances that he was owned, and in 1642 had a commission for a Captain of Foot in King Charles the First's army." Are there any records of his career after entering the army ?

During the preparation of this work for the press, a strange and sad chapter has been added to the annals of Malmesbury. Mr. Walter Powell, a native of the town and for some years its representative in Parliament, acquired considerable celebrity as a bold and skilful aeronaut. On Saturday, Dec. 10, 1881, he ascended from Bath in the Government balloon Saladin, accompanied by Captain James Templer and Mr. A. Agg-Gardner. On attempting, about five o'clock, to descend near Weymouth, Captain Templer and Mr. Agg-Gardner were thrown from the car, the latter sustaining a fracture of the leg; while the lightened balloon suddenly rising carried Mr. Powell out to sea in the gathering darkness of a December night. Days of anxious search and enquiry followed, but the only certain information obtained was the discovery on the coast of a thermometer which had formed part of the balloon furniture.

Mr. Powell, who was unmarried, had a large circle of friends, by whom he was much beloved and admired; and as a Parliamentary representative he was exceedingly popular, not only among his political supporters, but among his fellow townsmen in general.

Tradition credits the large parish of *Sherstone*, lying five miles west of Malmesbury, with a redoubtable champion, bearing an undignified name; but laden with honours and rewards. Aubrey writes:—"*Mem:* The old woemen and children have these verses by tradition, viz. :—

'Fight well Rattlebone
Thou shalt have Sherstone.'
'What shall I with Sherstone doe
Without I have all things thereto?'
'Thou shalt have Wych and Willesly,
Easton towne and Pinkeney.',

In the wall of the Church Porch on the outside in a nich without inscription or escutcheon, is a little figure about 2 foote and a half high, ill done, which they call *Rattle Bone*, who, the tradition is, did much service against the Danes, when they infested this part of the countrey." Archæologists can trace no connection between this figure and the legendary hero whom the Sherstone people still delight to honour.

South of Sherstone, and lying on the borders of Gloucestershire, is the little village of *Aldrington alias Alderton*, as

THOMAS GORE,

the old antiquary, was accustomed to write it. Here he was born, and here, during the stirring events of the seventeenth century, he lived, largely absorbed in the study of Heraldry and Genealogy; and in the collection of antiquities, and those of "all sorts." He was of ancient family, was educated at Oxford, and went to Lincoln's Inn ; but appears to have lived chiefly on his estates. He was at one time on intimate terms with Aubrey, a friendship probably resulting from some congeniality of tastes and pursuits. He was Sheriff of the County in 1680, and died in 1684. His pedantic and curious Will is given by Canon Jackson, in Vol. XIV. of the "Wiltshire Magazine."

A glimpse of the brave and hearty martyr-bishop,

HUGH LATIMER,

is always interesting ; and Aubrey gives us one at *West Kington*, a few miles south of Alderton, and close to Gloucestershire. " Bp. Latimer," he says, " was rector here. In the walk at the Parsonage House is a little scrubbed hollow Oak called " Latimer's Oak,—where he used to sit." To this too brief note Canon Jackson adds the following information :— " Hugh Latimer was instituted to this Rectory in 1530 by the celebrated Cardinal Campegio, then Bishop of Sarum. He remained about five years. His letters to Sir Edward Baynton, of Bromham, are written from this place. In them he speaks of his ' little Bishoprick of West Kington ;' of the ' Lord of Farley,' and in another letter, ' As for pilgrimage, you would wonder what juggling there is to get money withal. I dwell within half a mile of the Fossway, and you would wonder to see how they come by flocks out of the west country to many images, but chiefly to the blood of Hailes.' " (Hales Abbey, near Winchcomb, Gloucestershire.)

The church, which is of Early English date, was restored in 1856, by the exertions of the Rev. G. N. Barrow, then rector. Latimer's pulpit is preserved ; and on the south side of the chancel a stained glass window has been erected to his memory, at the cost of Mr. G. W. Gabriel, of Bristol, the architect of the Church restoration. It represents the reformer standing under an oak, holding a crozier in one hand and a Bible in the other ; and is inscribed, " Hugh Latimer, Bishop and Martyr, sometime Rector of this Parish."

With *Castle Combe* the Scropes were long associated. This family came into Wilts from Yorkshire.

SIR WILLIAM LE SCROPE, FIRST EARL OF WILTSHIRE,

who was the eldest son of Lord Scrope, of Bolton, obtained the grant of the Castle and Town of Marlborough from Richard II. in 1894. He filled many high offices in the service of that monarch, and in 1398 was appointed Lord Treasurer. On the landing of the Duke of Lancaster—Henry IV.— Earl Scrope, adhering to the cause of Richard, took refuge in Bristol Castle. Here he was besieged by Henry, and being taken prisoner was beheaded without trial July 30, 1899. Whatever may have been his loyalty to his king, his character as a statesman is open to much reproach. Shakespeare pillories him in the line—

> " The Earl of Wiltshire hath this Realm in farm."

He died childless. His brothers Roger and Stephen, marrying two daughters of Robert, Lord Tibetot, came into possession of estates at Castle Combe which the family continued to hold for nearly five centuries, furnishing many names of eminence in Wiltshire history.

WILLIAM SCROPE,

the last male descendant of this famous family, is known in sporting circles as the author of two much admired books : *Days of Deer Stalking*, and *Days and Nights of Salmon Fishing*. His classical attainments and literary ability, together with his keen appreciation of nature, enabled him to treat these subjects with such felicity that some critics rank his works with Walton's *Angler* and Davy's *Salmonia*. He was also an artist of no mean powers, the skill of his pencil being little inferior to that of his pen. His death in the 81st year of his age occurred in July, 1852.

The son-in-law of this gentleman,

GEORGE POULETT SCROPE,

the last bearer of this ancient name, will be long and honourably remembered. This gentleman, whose own family name was Thompson, was born in 1797, and on the side of his mother was of Wiltshire blood. He married in 1821, Emma Phipps, only daughter of William Scrope, Esq., and thereupon took the name and arms of Scrope in lieu of Thompson by royal license. The Liberal constituency of Stroud elected him in May, 1833; and he retained his seat in Parliament till 1837, when he retired. Mr. Scrope was the author of several able pamphlets on political, scientific, and archæological subjects, including *A History of Castle Combe*. After the death of his wife he sold his Castle Combe estate and removed to Fairlawn, near Cobham, Surrey, where he died 18th January, 1876.

Kington St. Michael is on many accounts a notable parish. S. Mary's Priory, which stood about three quarters of a mile north of the parish church, on a site now occupied by a farm house, was for centuries a flourishing religious institution. Founded probably in the twelfth century, it continued in existence till the dissolution. Aubrey, who appears to have obtained his information from good sources, has given an interesting account of the nuns. "Old Jacques," he says, "who lived where Charles Hadnam did, could see from his house the Nuns of the Priory of St. Mary's Kington come forth into the Nymph-Hay" (a large ground on the east side of the House) "with their rocks and wheels to spin, and with their sewing work. He would say that he hath told threescore and ten, but of Nuns there were not so many, but in all, with Lay-sisters, as widows, old maids, and young girls, there might be such a number." The last Prioress was Mary Dennis, who was pensioned with £5 a year. She died at Bristol in 1523, "a good olde maide, verie vertuose and godlye."

Easton Piers, a small tything in this parish, was the birthplace of

JOHN AUBREY,

the earliest topographical historian of his native county. His father, Richard Aubrey, of Broadchalk, a gentleman of good estate, married Deborah, daughter of Isaac Lyte, of Easton Piers, where, Aubrey tells us, he "was borne about sun-rising, on March 12 (St. Gregory's day), A.D. 1625. In an ill hour, Saturn directly opposing my ascendant, in my Grandfather's chamber, I first drew my breath: very weak and like to dye, and therefore christened that morning before morning prayer." From loose and vague notes found among his MSS. some autobiographical facts have been arranged by Canon Jackson. Of these we shall make use in our brief sketch of his life.

"1629. About 3 years old I had a grievous ague, I can remember it. I got not health till eleven or twelve. This sickness nipt my strength in the bud. When a boy, bred ignorant at Eston, was very curious; greatest delight to be with the artificers that came there, joyners, carpenters, cowpers, masons, and understand their trades. *Horis vacuis* (at leisure hours), I drew and painted. Did ever love to converse with old men as Living Histories; cared not for play. Anno 1633. I entered into my Grammar at the Latin School, at Yatton Keynell, in the Church, where the Curate, Mr. Hart, taught the eldest boys Virgil, Ovid, &c. I remember having learnt the Alphabet from a Horn book, now extinct. 1634. Afterwards I went to School to Mr. Robert Latimer, a delicate and little person, Rector of Leigh Delamere—a mile—fine walk. When a boy never riotous or prodigal: of inventive and philosophical head; my witt was always working, but not to verse. Exceeding mild of spirit, mighty susceptible of fascination. Strong and early impulse to Antiquities. 1642, May 3. Entered at Trinity Coll. Oxon. Now did Bellona thunder: and as a clear sky is sometimes overstretched with a dismall black cloud, so was the serene peace by the Civil War through the factions of those times. In August following, 1643, my Father sent for me home for feare."

After three years of what he calls " sad life in the country, spent chiefly with servants and rustiques and soldiers," Aubrey was admitted of Middle Temple. By the death of his father his legal studies, which had been much interrupted, were brought to an end. In succeeding to his paternal estates he suffered heavy losses in vexatious litigation; but for some years possessed a good income. He now gave himself to antiquarian and historical pursuits, forming friendships with many learned men, including Hobbes and Anthony Wood; and in his own way working very industriously. He visited Ireland and France; was shipwrecked; suffered many misfortunes (all of which he attributed to the evil influence of the planet Saturn, under which he was born); and was reduced to indigent circumstances. Amidst all these events he had many love adventures in which he experienced some " hair breadth escapes from matrimony," His own confession that he was "mighty susceptible of fascination" may throw some light upon the numerous love affairs in which he was from time to time engaged. In 1650 he speaks of being "suitor to Mistress Jane Codrington ;" the next year he writes "About the 16th or 18th April I saw that incomparable good conditioned gentlewoman, Mistress M. Wiseman, with whom at first sight I was in love." His next memorandum strangely couples love and law. "1656. This year and the last was a strange yeare to me. Several love and law suites." He next writes as a bereaved and disappointed lover ;—"1657. Nov. 27, Obiit Domina Kasker Ryves, with whom I was to marry : to my great losse—£2000 ; besides counting one of her Brothers £1000 per ann." His next attempt was still more unfortunate. "1665. Nov. 1. I made my first address (in an ill hour) to Joan Sumner," of Seend. The course of love brought the parties into the law courts, and even led to Aubrey's temporary arrest.

It was, however, in a lady that he found a true friend in his days of adversity. Under the hospitable roof of Lady Long, of Draycote House, he dwelt in quietness and comfort, diligently pursuing his favourite studies. It was while journeying on one occasion, from London to Draycote, that he was taken ill at Oxford, where he died in 1697. He was buried in the church of St. Mary Magdalene, the Register of which records : "1697. John Aubrey, a stranger, was buried June 7."

His work *An Essay towards the Description of the North Division of Wiltshire* has been corrected and enlarged by Canon Jackson, and published as *The Topographical Collections of John Aubrey, F.R.S., The Natural History of Wiltshire*, another of his works, replete with curious and entertaining facts and suggestions, has been ably edited by Mr. Britton, and published by the Wiltshire Topographical Society. In addition to these, he wrote *Lives of Eminent Men*, and also a *History of Surrey*, a county in which he resided for some years. Shrewd and observant as he was, he was yet led by his credulity into many inaccuracies and absurdities ; and he has been often ridiculed for the idle tales of apparitions and miraculous events which he relates. In these respects Aubrey was no weaker than his contemporaries, nearly all of whom were believers in witches and ghosts. Even John Wesley, who lived a hundred years later, was equally credulous, and his journal contains more supernatural tales and fancies than can be found in Aubrey's writings. The harshest judgment of our Wiltshire author is that of Anthony Wood, who after twenty-five years acquaintance, not only treated him unhandsomely, but said of him spitefully, "He was a shiftless person, roving and magotie-headed, and something little better than crazed; and being exceedingly credulous, would stuff his many letters to A. W. with folleries and mis-informations." But, as Professor Morley says, "Anthony Wood had not a sweet temper, and was accustomed to speak his mind roughly." Canon Jackson, whose estimate of the old Collector's labours is generous and favourable, approvingly quotes the words of a reviewer in reference to his "Lives of Eminent Men." "For this and many like treasures of literary gossip, we account Aubrey, despite of his love of ghosts and wonderful accidents, among the benefactors of mankind."

A remarkable successor to Aubrey appeared in

JOHN BRITTON,

who, singular to say, was born in Kington St. Michael, within a mile of the chamber where Aubrey first drew breath, on July 7th, 1771. His father was a baker, shopkeeper, and small farmer. There was a large family—ten children in all, and the poor parents had to make sore struggles for a living. The education of the children was not, however, neglected, and John was sent to school till he was thirteen. His services were then required at home, and for three years he carried round the bread to out-lying customers, and otherwise assisted his over-worked and over-burdened parents. But the evil day came; the father lost his reason, the mother died broken-hearted, and the children had to be dispersed among their friends. John fell into the hands of an uncle in London, by whom he was apprenticed for six years to the landlord of the Jerusalem Tavern, Clerken-well, to work in the wine cellar. It was an uncongenial and unhealthy employment, from which he was at length released six months before the term of his apprenticeship had expired. His only comforts through this period of dreary servitude had been books, which he diligently read; and the smiles of a young woman employed in the tavern, with whom he had fallen in love. On leaving the wine cellars his unjust master, who had engaged to pay him twenty pounds, gave him two, as through ill health he was unable to complete his full time. Poor and weakly, he naturally turned to his uncles—he had two in London—but neither would give him a bed or a meal. The world was now before him, and the friendless youth had to shape his own course. The series of adventures and struggles which followed, were such as Dickens would have wrought into a volume of humour and pathos. Following the lass on whom his heart was set he travelled to Plympton in Devonshire. It was labour in vain ; he met with a refusal, and returned to London shirtless, shoeless, and penniless. But he bore up bravely, obtained employment, and with cheerful heart pursued his course. He read, wrote, sang, attended debating clubs, and in a variety of ways stored his mind and sharpened his wits. His surroundings were often far from refined and pure, yet amidst all he gained some polish, and preserved, as he did in after life, a moral character free from reproach. At length he entered on literature as a profession, and for nearly sixty years continued to work with an amount of industry and ability that excites wonder and admiration. His first great work, *Beauties of Wiltshire*, appeared in two volumes, in 1801, and was soon followed by others worthy of his pen. In 1814 he commenced *Cathedral Antiquities* of England, a magnificent work in 14 volumes, which was not completed till 1835. In the meanwhile he published a third volume of his *Beauties of Wiltshire*. Canon Jackson, after giving a classified list of his works, presents the following totals of their number, pages, engravings, and amount of money expended in their production :—57 volumes, besides essays ; containing 17,254 printed pages ; illustrated with 1867 engravings, and issued at a cost of £50,328. But what arithmetic can tell us the amount of time, mental and manual labour, care and anxiety which these productions must have involved ? Seldom has public money been more deservedly applied than the pension of £75 a year devoted to this indefatigable and useful writer in the Chancellorship of Mr. Disraeli.

The occasion of his seventy-fourth birthday anniversary was celebrated in a manner which proved the high esteem in which he was held. He was entertained at dinner at the Castle Hotel, Richmond, by a party of eighty-two gentlemen, by whom it was resolved that he should be presented with some permanent testimonial. A sum of £1,000 was accordingly raised, and this, at his own suggestion, was employed in the preparation of an *Autobiography*. This "curious and instructive memoir" consists of two volumes; and shows, to use his own words, " how much may be effected by zeal and industry, with moderate talents and without academic learning." Some things which he could not, without breach of modesty, say of himself, are thus said of him :—" He had an active and penetrating mind, remarkable power of arrangement, an excellent memory, a kind heart, and a moral character free from reproach. He was simple in his habits, fond of children and a favourite with them ; a great lover of Natural History, and an advocate of mercy to the humblest animal."

His prolonged vigour of mind and body were thus referred to by himself when addressing the Wiltshire Archæological Society at Devizes, in 1853 : —" It is usually thought that in old age all the physical and mental powers of man become torpid and insensible. Whatever may be the case in other instances, I can venture to assert that in my 83rd year my nervous and bodily system is as susceptible of pain, while my sensibilities are as acute, as they were in days of youth. . . . Time never seems to flag, days are too short for the duties and gratifications which every succeeding morning presents, and *ennui* is unknown in my personal vocabulary."

His long and active life closed January 1, 1857, so that he was in his eighty-sixth year. A singularly appropriate monument marks his grave in Norwood cemetery. It consists of a large unwrought monolith of Bramley-fallstone, similar in form to those at Stonehenge. This stands upon a plinth of the same material, on which his name and dates of birth and death are inscribed.

The names of Aubrey and Britton have been happily associated in a memorial window in their native parish church. A brass plate placed beneath it at the expense of Canon Jackson bears the following inscription ; —" At the Restoration of this Church, A.D. 1857, this Window was erected by Public Subscription to commemorate two Natives of this parish, alike distinguished by their writings on the Antiquities of Wiltshire. JOHN AUBREY, F.R.S., born at Easton Piers, March 12th, 1625, died at

Oxford, June 1697; and John Britton, F.A.S., born at Kington St. Michael, July 7th, 1771, died in London January 1st, 1857.

"Laus Deo."

Draycot Cerne reminds us of a well-known old Wiltshire family. "The Longs," wrote Aubrey, "are now the most flourishing and numerous family in the county." His references to them are numerous. In one place he tells us "Old Sir Walter Long, grandfather to Colonel Long, kept a trumpeter, and rode with xxx servants and retainers to Marleborough," and elsewhere relates how this same Sir Walter was the first to introduce the practice of tobacco smoking into Wiltshire. Like many others, the old baronet engaged in an unsuccessful mining enterprise, which is thus told :—" About the beginning of the raigne of King James the First, Sir Walter Long, of Dracot, digged for silver a deep pitt, through blew clay, and gott five pounds worth, for sixty pounds charges or more. It was on the west end of the stable; but I doubt there was a cheat put upon him." Aubrey may well say, " 'Tis some satisfaction to know where a minerall is *not*."

Henry, a younger brother of Sir Walter, was murdered under singular circumstances, in 1594. Some quarrel, of which nothing is now known, appears to have existed between him and Sir Charles and Sir Henry Danvers, sons of Sir John Danvers, of Dauntsey. On Friday, October 4, Mr. Long, with his brother Sir Walter, and several other gentlemen, was dining about twelve o'clock at one Chamberlayne's house, probably a tavern, in Corsham, when the two Danverses, accompanied by a number of their retainers, burst into the room and shot him dead. The murderers, both of whom were quite young men, being twenty-three and twenty-two years of age respectively, escaped on horseback to the Earl of Southampton's, and soon after crossed to Brittany. They were outlawed by the coroner's inquisition : but even while this sentence was in force Sir Henry was made a peer, and soon afterwards it was entirely reversed, so that the perpetrators of this crime altogether escaped punishment. Sir Charles was beheaded in 1600, for joining the Earl of Essex in his plot against Queen Elizabeth. Of Sir Henry, whose after career was one of great distinction, we shall speak further when we come to Dauntsey.

Of Sir James Long, Aubrey speaks in high terms as "my ever honoured friend, whom I name for honour's sake." Sir James, as a magistrate, had to do with the prosecution of a number of unhappy old creatures who were suspected in that superstitious age of witchcraft. The brief story as told by Aubrey is very terrible :—"About 167— there was a cabal of witches detected at Malmsbury; they were examined by Sir James Long, of Draycot Cerne, and by him committed to Salisbury gaol. I think there were seven or eight old women hanged. There were odd things sworne against them, as the strange manner of the dyeing of H. Denny's horse, and of flying in the air on a staffe. These examinations Sir James hath fairly written in a book, which he promised to give to the Royall Societie." This was little more than two hundred years ago ! The names of many other members of the family are closely interwoven with Wiltshire history, and are connected with several localities besides Draycot.

Charles Edward Long, Esq., a well-known associate of the Wiltshire Archæological Society, and a frequent contributor to the pages of its magazine, appears to have been a descendant of this ancient house. While not putting himself forward as " of the undoubted blood and lineage of the knightly race of Wraxhall and Draycot," yet his Wiltshire origin and family traditions pointed to that conclusion. He died September 25, 1861, aged 65 years. A brief memoir by Canon Jackson appeared in the Wiltshire Magazine, vol. vii., and is filled with facts relative to his life and works.

One of the seventeenth century vicars of *Sutton Benger*, " Parson"

WILLIAM NOBLE,

appears to have indulged in verse-making. Aubrey gives several poetical epitaphs from monuments in Aldrington Church, which bear his name. One on a friend's child four years of age is full of sweetness and consolation :—

> " So rare a piece of beauty, grace and witt,
>   Though God hath shewed us, ye he thought not fit
>   For us to gaze upon too long : 'twas He
>   That tooke her to himself, himself to see.
>   Admired she was by all who did behold her ;
>   Much more shall be when God anew shall mould her."

There is a puritanic ring about all these compositions.

Brief, but interesting, are some notes which Mr. Robert Brewin has supplied concerning

JOHN FRY,

an ancestor of the once well known London bankers, of the firm " Fry and Co." This John Fry, who was living a hundred years ago, in Sutton Benger, was a member of the Society of Friends. He was engaged in business as a general shopkeeper. Influenced by a religious spirit and possessing the faculty of rhyming, he composed and published a volume of verses which he entitled *Select Poems, containing Religious Epistles, &c., occasionally written on various subjects, to which is added the History of Elijah and Elisha ; by John Fry.* The Preface is dated " Sutton Benger, in Wilts, 25 Third Month, 1774." "A new edition with additions," containing 262 pages, and treating of about 30 subjects, was published in 1793. One of George Herbert's proverbs says, " Between the business of life and the day of death, a space ought to be interposed." The thoughtful old Friend seems to have been of the same opinion, as he was out of business and enjoying the calm and comfort of retirement, when he wrote in prosaic style, but in words likely to be remembered :—

> " Retired from trade to a still quiet life,
> With only one servant, myself, and my wife ;
> A state betwixt ease and constant employ,
> Is a state I should choose, and a state I enjoy."

We have no particulars of the future course and close of this " still quiet life," but would hope that the way continued smooth and that the end was peace.

Somewhat over a hundred years ago a grave and intelligent looking young man, of quiet deportment and plain attire, was often seen in *Christian Malford.* He was there known as one of the preachers engaged in the great religious revival of that period. He afterwards became known not only through Wilts and Gloucestershire—but in London and far distant parts of the kingdom, as Cornelius Winter —a convert and *protégé* of Whitefield ; a friend and fellow-worker of Rowland Hill ; the tutor of William Jay ; and a man of remarkable character and influence. At the period referred to he was itinerating with a most imperfect education, with no regular stipend, and with nothing like a "certain dwelling-place."

"I felt the importance of a place to retire in," he says, "and groaned under the want of improvement. My efforts were frequently discovered, and as frequently reproached by the enemies of literature: and our connexions abounded with those who made little discrimination between study and sin. I furnished a room in the cottage at Christian Malford, adjoining a malthouse which had been converted into a preaching place, of which I was extremely fond, and where I had an inclination to live and die. For this room I paid rent; here I collected my little library and papers, resorted to it as often and staid as long as I could, but as I paid for all I had, and my purse contained shillings rather than guineas, I could not continue there long at a time. It being unto me whenever I could get there a heaven upon earth, it may be supposed I left it with reluctance." Mr. Winter was ordained minister of three religious societies then meeting respectively at Christian Malford, Castle Combe, and Chippenham. In 1778 he became pastor of the Independent Congregation at Marlborough, and ten years afterwards removed to Painswick in Gloucestershire where he died beloved and honoured, in 1808.

It would be ungrateful to tread the causeway leading through the parishes of Langley Burrell, Kellaways, and Tytherton, to Chippenham Cliff, a distance of over four miles, without mention of

MAUD HEATH.

It was an old saying that he does a good work who builds a church or a bridge. Men have been thankful for smaller benefits. A seat by a road-side in Lincolnshire called forth the following *impromptu*:

> "God bless thee, Charley Anderson,
> For making here a seat,
> That travellers may sit upon,
> And rest their weary feet."

And a village well in Devonshire bears this quaint inscription:—

> "God be thanket that William Pranket,
> In the year seventeen hundred and one,
> Did cause this water here to run."

What then shall be said of Maud Heath, who having been a market woman, and often sorely felt the toil and inconvenience of travelling on a bad road from Kington Burrell to Chippenham, devoted her hard earned savings to the construction and maintenance of this causeway? Upright stones at different parts of the way bear suitable inscriptions. The first, at Wick Hill, says—

> "From this Wick Hill begins the praise
> Of Maud Heath's gift to these highways."

That at the Chippenham end informs us—

> "Hither extendeth Maud Heath's gift,
> For where I stand is Chippenham Clift.
> Erected in 1698 : given in 1474."

While that at Kellaways bears this fuller record :—

"To the memory of the worthy Maud Heath, of Langley Burrell, Spinster, who in the year of grace 1474, for the good of travellers, did in charity bestow in land and houses about eight pounds a year, for ever, to be laid out on the highway and causey leading from Wick Hill to Chippenham Clift."

An iron bridge erected by this fund crosses the Avon at Kellaways, and a raised path, upon 64 arches, enables travellers in the time of floods, which are frequent here, to pass the stream in safety.

The story of Maud Heath " being an old goody market woman, or at the highest, a farm-housekeeper, is the favourite one," says Canon Jackson, who suggests some doubts as to its correctness ; "and," he adds, "is now likely to be perpetuated. For the tradition has been most substantially personified in a bodily form and of a material likely to endure, as long as the causey itself shall last." The reference here is to the figure of Maud herself "in the full egg and butter uniform, or what is supposed to be such, of *temp.* Edward IV. ; upon her head a heavy coiffure, in her hand a staff, and by her side a basket." This said figure sits upon a column of freestone forty feet high, erected on Bremhill Wick Hill, at the cost of Henry, Marquis of Lansdowne, and William Lisle Bowles, Vicar of Bremhill : the latter of whom also supplied the following lines as part of the inscription :—

c

"Thou who dost pause on this aerial height,
Where MAUD HEATH'S Pathway winds in shade or light.
Christian wayfarer, in a world of strife,
Be still—and ponder on the path of life."

We must not pass the little village of *Tytherton Lucas* without honourable mention of the Rev.

HENRY BRINDLEY,

who was rector here from 1785 to 1819, and who left a guinea a year for a sermon to be preached against cruelty to animals.

WILLIAM BARRETT,

the Historian of Bristol, belonged to a family of, or near Chippenham. He was born 1735, and was probably a native of this parish. His name figures in the strange and melancholy story of the boy-poet Chatterton.

The flourishing town of *Chippenham*, situated on the Bristol Avon which runs here from Christian Malford on its way to Melksham, furnishes us with the name of

DR. JOHN SCOTT,

a learned divine, who was born here in 1638. He was the son of a grazier, and served an apprenticeship of three years in London. Abandoning trade he went as a student to Oxford. Having entered into holy orders he successively became minister of three London parishes, and was also made a prebendary of St. Paul's and a Canon of Windsor. A bishopric was offered him, but this he declined from unwillingness to take the oath of homage. Strenuously opposing the progress of Popery in the time of James II., he gave vigorous support to the Revolution, and was rewarded by William III. with the rich rectory of St. Giles-in-the-Fields. He died in 1694, and was buried in his own church. He was a man of high character and good ability. His chief work is entitled, " *The Christian Life ; from its beginning to its consummation in glory.*"

Chippenham is indebted to several benefactors whose names and works are worthy of record. Six residences, standing on the Bristol-road, built and endowed by Charles Bailey, Esq., furnish homes for aged and infirm medical men or their widows. To the late Joseph Neeld, Esq., of Grittleton, who was for many years member for the borough, Chippenham owes the Town-hall, the covered Market-yard, the Exchange-room, and other public buildings in High-street, which were his munificent gifts. Nor must we fail to name Messrs. Thomas Mills and Son, whose disinterested efforts raised a sum of nearly £1400 for the erection of the handsome Temperance-hall, which stands upon the site of an old inn known as the "White Hart."

After these worthy names we hesitate to mention one which was notorious two hundred years ago, and has come down to us in the name of the fanatical sect which its bearer founded. Ludowic Muggleton was a native of Chippenham, and by trade a tailor. Dr. South, referring to the Revelation and its expositors, somewhat irreverently said that it was a book which found a man mad or made him so. We do not know how it was in the case of Muggleton, but there can be little doubt that he was a madman if he was not a vile impostor. He and a companion, one John Reeve, proclaimed themselves to be Moses and Aaron, and also the two witnesses described in the eleventh chapter of the mysterious Apocalypse. They soon found believers, and the Muggletonians became one of the many sects with which that period swarmed. Under the intolerant and barbarous laws of those times, Muggleton was pilloried and imprisoned, and his trashy books were burnt by the hangman. These absurd and cruel measures neither effected his reformation nor destroyed his influence. He died 1697, aged 90 years.

It is discreditable to Macaulay that he ranks Muggleton with George Fox. It is associating darkness with light. Muggleton had no sturdier opponents than the Quakers. Richard Farnsworth was one and William Penn another. Penn's book, *The New Witnesses proved Old Hereticks*, contains not only elaborate arguments, but also gives accounts of two interviews he had with Muggleton. Here we get a view of the prophet :— "At my second visit to him (in company of a friend)" says Penn, "I found him sitting by the Chimney Corner quaffing with some of his. Followers and Benefactors, as what we saw before us did evidence. My first salute was thus :—*W.P.* How is it Ludowick ?   Methinks thou look'st with thy old threadbare black suit, like a sequestered begging Priest.

M. I am a Priest.

W.P. Of what Order ?

M. The Order of Aaron.

W.P. Aaron ! where are thy bells ?

M. I have them in mystery, &c."

In forwarding a copy of this work, Penn wrote a letter addressed "For Ludowick Muggleton, an Accuser of the Brethren, False Prophet and Impostor;" and in which he tells him "The sense of thy ungodly and Blasphemous Practices (though otherwise an Adversary of little Moment) and their influence upon some poor, miserable, dark, and ignorant souls, begot in me a Desire to Detect thee, &c."

Canon Jackson refers to another work, written by some other author, and bearing the title of *A Modest Account of the wicked Life of that Grand Impostor Ludowick Muggleton.*   It sets forth " all the memorable actions that he did and all the strange accidents which have befallen him, ever since his first coming to London, to the 25th day of January, 1676."   It also gives " the reasons which first drew him to those damnable principles ; with several pleasant stories concerning him ; proving his commission to be but counterfeit, and himself a cheat."

Among the many centenarians named in Wiltshire records, one of the most remarkable was Anne Simms, of *Studley Green*, in the parish of Chippenham, who died in 1785, aged 113 years.   A newspaper of the time said :—" Till within a few months of her death, she was able to walk to and from the seat of the Marquis of Lansdown, near three miles from Studley.   She had been, and continued, till upwards of 100 years of age, the most noted poacher in that part of the country ; and frequently boasted of selling to gentlemen, the fish taken out of their own ponds.   Her coffin and shroud she had purchased, and kept in her apartment more than 20 years."

Cooke describes *Corsham* as " one of the most pleasant villages" in the whole county.   "The air," he says, " is so particularly clear and salubrious that the inhabitants in general live to a very advanced age.   This, indeed, appears from the inscriptions on the gravestones in the churchyard, many being from 80 to 90, and several upwards of 100." In further proof of this he tells the following incredible tale which he says he heard from some of the inhabitants. "Some years ago, an eminent physician who was going to Bath, having put up at an inn in the village, was accosted by some beggars of both sexes; and being curious to know how old they were, one of them answered him that he was about a hundred, and that another standing near him was six score. The doctor expressed great surprise, on which the beggar added, that the preceding Christmas there was a morris-dance at a neighbouring gentleman's house, when ten of those mendicants performed their parts with great agility, whose ages, when put together, amounted to upwards of one thousand years."

The name of

SIR RICHARD BLACKMORE,

a native of *Corsham*, was at one time prominent in medical, literary, and political circles. Born during the Commonwealth, and sent to Westminster School at the age of thirteen, he entered Edmund Hall, Oxford, in 1668. He directed his attention to the study of medicine, obtained a Doctor's degree at Padua, and returning to London became a member of the College of Physicians in 1687. His political opinions procured his advancement. William III. appointed him one of his physicians, and afterwards honoured him with knighthood. Under Queen Anne he retained his post as one of the royal physicians, till he at length resigned it. The professional duties of a large practice did not prevent his engagement in literary pursuits. Poem after poem—heroic, religious, and satirical—flowed from his busy, if not brilliant pen, meeting with favour from the public, but incurring the bitter criticism of some contemporary bards. Addison and Johnson have estimated his productions much more favourably—especially praising his "*Creation: a philosophical poem*," from which many fine passages might be quoted. His hostile critics receive a keen reproof in Johnson's remark that the poet provoked their enmity more by his virtues than his dullness. He attempted *A New Version of the Psalms of David, fitted to the Tunes used in Churches.* This was a failure. "Blackmore's name," says Johnson, "must be added to those of many others who by the same attempt have obtained only the praise of meaning well." His writings on medical, political, and theological subjects were also numerous, but not of lasting interest. He died in 1729.

DR. EDMUND WELLS,

another native of this little town, and a contemporary of Blackmore, was educated at Westminster School and Christ Church College, Oxford. He took his D.D. degree at this University and was appointed Greek Professor. Having obtained the living of Cotesbach, Leicestershire, he passed the remainder of his life in that parish, where he died in 1730, aged 65. Among his writings were some pamphlets against nonconformists; an answer to Dr. Clarke on the Trinity, and some educational works on Mathematics and Geography.

The Methuen family, of Corsham Court, trace their descent from an ancestor who came with Edgar Atheling from Hungary to England, and afterwards settled in Scotland, in the reign of William I. He received the barony of Methuen, in Perthshire, from Malcolm Conmore, the Scottish king, and from this place the family surname was assumed. In the reign of Elizabeth one of the descendants who favoured the Reformation sought refuge from persecution in England. He found favour in the eyes of the Queen, and his eldest son, who was in the Church, obtained some valuable preferments in Somersetshire. Paul Methuen, a grandson of this clergyman, possessed property at Bradford-on-Avon, where he became eminent as one of the greatest clothiers of his day. His son John, of Bishop's Cannings, was representative for Devizes, and Lord Chancellor of Ireland in the reigns of William III. and Queen Anne. He died in 1706, leaving a son,

SIR PAUL METHUEN,

born in 1672, who may be ranked among the most distinguished public men of his time. He filled important offices of State, and was especially famous as an ambassador, in which character he appeared at many foreign courts. He was an accomplished linguist, and was extensively read in the

best authors, while his taste in works of art was acknowledged by his contemporaries and is proved by his valuable collection of paintings with which
the galleries of Corsham Court are now adorned. Voltaire and Steele
speak his praises. Anecdotes are told of his personal courage, particularly
one relating how he voluntarily took part in a sea fight and narrowly
escaped drowning. He lived a bachelor, professing to esteem wedlock as a
happiness of which he was not worthy; a reason which was probably
thought more complimentary than satisfactory by the fair sex. He died
April 11, 1757, and was buried close to his father in Westminster Abbey
Church.

A gallant act performed by a present member of the family was reported
from Berlin in January, 1881. Colonel Methuen, then Military Attaché to
the British Embassy at that court, at great personal risk to himself, rescued
a man who was drowning amidst masses of broken ice in the Canal. The
deed, which elicited the applause of all who witnessed it, was subsequently
acknowledged by the Emperor himself, who in the presence of all the
Diplomatic Corps, at a grand Court ball, presented Colonel Methuen with
the much coveted Prussian silver medal " for rescuing from peril."

It was in the neighbourhood of Corsham that Capt. Speke, the great
African traveller and the discoverer of Lake Nyanza, one of the principal
sources of the Nile, met his death by the accidental discharge of his own
gun on Sept. 15, 1864. His enterprising and useful life closed at the
age of 41.

The parish of *Box*, long famed for its stone quarries, has also become
famous for its railway tunnel mid-way between Corsham and Bath, on the
Great Western line. This great work was among the earlier achievements
of railway enterprise and engineering skill. It was commenced in 1836,
and completed in 1841. Its length is one mile and three-quarters, its
height forty feet, and its width thirty. The north-east opening is just
below Corsham, and the tunnel passes for some distance through the great
oolite formation, but afterwards enters fuller's earth, and pursues its course
through inferior oolite, blue marl, and lias limestone. Heavy discourage-
ments and great difficulties were encountered in its construction, but the
skill of Mr. Brunel, the engineer, and the energy and scientific ability of

Messrs. Brewer and Lewis, the contractors, brought the stupendous undertaking to a successful close. The work of excavation was commenced at each end, and also from eleven intermediate shafts, and so admirable were the arrangements that the proposed lines of operation were worked out with scarcely an inch of deviation. No fewer than five hundred men were employed in its formation, and six steam engines were used for lifting the water and rubbish. The total progress was about six feet a day.

Chapel Playster, in this parish, near the meeting of several roads, was, says Aubrey, "heretofore a place of entertainment for Pilgrims that went to Glastonbury, to St. Joseph of Arimathea's Chapell. It is now an alehouse. On the outside towards the highway, is, in the wall, a place for holy water." It afterwards became the head quarters of a notorious highwayman, John Poulter, *alias* Baxter, who according to tradition, made a window commanding a view of the Corsham road so as to be ready for arrivals. His career ended on the gallows at Salisbury.

The parish of *Lacock* supplies numerous subjects for the pen of the archæologist. Before the Reformation it was a place of some ecclesiastical importance. Many families of distinction, notably the Sheringtons, Baynards, Montagus, and Talbots have resided within its boundaries. Of a lady of the Sherington family, Aubrey, in his chapter of *Men and Women*, tells a romantic story, doubtless based upon some facts. "Dame Olave, a daughter and co-heire of Sir [Henry] Sharington, of Lacock, being in love with [John] Talbot, a younger brother of the Earle of Shrewsbury, and her father not consenting that she should marry him, discoursing with him one night from the battlements of the Abbey Church, said shee, 'I will leap downe to you,' her sweetheart replied he would catch her then, but he did not believe she would have done it. She leap't downe, and the wind, which was then high, came under her coates and did something break her fall. Mr. Talbot caught her in his arms, but she struck him dead; she cried for help, and he was with difficulty brought to life again. Her father told her that since she had made such a leap she should e'en marrie him. She was my honoured friend Colonel Sharington Talbot's grandmother, and died at her house at Lacock, about 1651, being about an hundred years old." Britton says that the heroine of this tale, Olave, or

Olivia Sherington, married John Talbot, Esq., of Salwarpe, in the county of Worcester, fourth in descent from John, second Earl of Shrewsbury. She inherited the Lacock estate from her father, and it has ever since remained the property of that branch of the Talbot family.

Aubrey's brief account of

WILLIAM YOKENEY

is worth transcribing. It is contained in his chapter on *Worthies*, and runs as follows:—" Will. Yokeney, a lutinist and a composer of songs, *e.g.*, of Colonel Lovelace's songs, &c., was born at Lacock, 1646 (an error as to date). Among other fine compositions of songs by Will. Yokeney, this following ought to be remembered, made 1646 or 1647, viz.,—

> What if the King should come to the city,
>   Would he be then received I trow ?
> Would the Parliament treat him with rigor or pity ?
>   Some doe think yea, but most doe think no, &c.

It is a lively, briske aire, and was played by the lowd musick when King Charles the Second made his entry into London at his restauration."

A fine old mansion which stood at Lackham, in this parish, was for some generations the family seat of the Montagus, many of whose monuments are in the church.

GEORGE MONTAGU,

who was born here in 1755, has obtained celebrity as one of the most eminent practical naturalists of his day, and is credited with having " rendered most important and lasting service to English Natural History." He entered the army while quite a youth ; two years afterwards married a young lady in Scotland, and was almost immediately ordered with his regiment to America. The unhappy war was going on, and amidst its painful scenes, which made and left sore impressions upon his tender though gallant spirit, the young officer found some relief in the pursuits of natural science. For such studies he had strong predilections, which were developed by the new natural scenes by which he was surrounded. Birds especially engaged his attention, and ornithology became one of his favourite subjects. He resolved ultimately, however, that his studies should be directed chiefly to the birds and zoology of Britain. He obtained a Captaincy in America, but shortly afterwards returned to England, and settled in Wilts, where he was appointed Lieutenant-Colonel of the county militia. Subsequently he removed to Knowle, in Devonshire, choosing that locality as affording by its greater nearness to the sea more opportunities for the prosecution of his inquiries in marine zoology. The results of his labours appear in his " *Ornithological Dictionary*," published in 1802; in his " *Testacea Britannica*," which came out the following year; and in numerous papers contributed to the Transactions of the Linnean Society. His death, which resulted from lock jaw following an injury to his foot by piercing it with a rusty nail, took place June 20, 1815. Of his character it is said—"he was remarkably punctual in his engagements, and just and upright in all the transactions of life." The Trustees of the British Museum secured his fine collection of birds at a cost of £3000.

A monument in Lacock Church to the memory of his son Frederick, who, at the age of 26, fell in the battle of Albuera, in 1811, bears a touching epitaph written by the sorrowing father.

A mile or so east of Lacock, and situated on the west side of the road from Chippenham to Devizes, is *Spye Park*. The house, according to tradition, was first erected at Corsham in the reign of Henry VIII., but afterwards removed and rebuilt here by the Bayntuns in 1650. In the reign of Charles II. it became the property and occasional residence of John Wilmot, Earl of Rochester. With the character and life of this nobleman many records have made us acquainted. Possessed of great natural gifts, and even some moral excellence, he yet sunk into shameless vice and profligacy. The favourite companion of the licentious king, and a chief leader of his corrupt court, he soon wasted his strength "in riotous living," and at the age of thirty was tottering on the brink of the grave. Of his sickness, repentance, and death Gilbert Burnet, Bishop of Salisbury, has written a deeply interesting narrative. He died in 1680 at the age of thirty-two.

JOHN FOWLER.

Mr. Edmund Ruck, of Purton Manor, writes:—" You will find no man born in this county since 1800 more deserving note than the late John Fowler, the inventor of the Steam Plough. Mr. Fowler was born near Melksham, and all who knew him looked on him as a pattern of a thorough Englishman." This gentleman, the son of John and Rebecca Fowler, was born at Elm Grove, near Melksham, in 1826. The family belonged to the Society of Friends. The father, who was an elder of this religious body, was the possessor of "a character which was in some respects an uncommon one." In his business pursuits, which were those of a banker, and in his religious and social relationships, " a straightforward simplicity was very conspicuous." "While a most marked peculiarity of his nature was that it was forcible, he was yet full of love and gentleness." The mother, who was a Minister, was a woman of excellent spirit, and most devoted to her family. Under the influences of home and a neighbouring private school, John received a sound and careful education.

When about seventeen he was placed with the late Mr. W. C. Bowly, of Cirencester, to acquire a knowledge of the flour milling business. Here he remained about two years, and during this period his love of mechanical pursuits seems to have been developed, and he commenced those investigations and experiments which greatly influenced his after life. On leaving Cirencester he spent some time at Middlesbrough, and then went into business in the firm of Fowler and Fry, at Bristol. He subsequently passed much time at Ipswich, and then returned to the north, where his chief work was accomplished. Here he married Elizabeth Lucy, fourth daughter of the late excellent Joseph Pease, of Darlington, and here he spent the remainder of his life. His works were at Leeds, his residence at Ackworth.

The following notes, for which we are indebted to the courtesy of Mr. H. A. Byng, of the Orwell Works, Ipswich, supply some interesting facts relative to the great invention with which Mr. Fowler's name is associated. Mr. Byng writes:—

"I first came in contact with Mr. Fowler, in 1849, at which time this firm (then styled Ransomes and May) were manufacturing his Draining Ploughs. For many years after that time, Mr. Fowler was endeavouring to reduce ploughing by steam to some practical shape, and had a great variety of experimental apparatus made here for the purpose. In all this preliminary work, Mr. Fowler had in the late Mr. William Worby (then one of the managers of the establishment) a most able and sympathizing coadjutor, and when at length Mr. Fowler conceived the idea of the balance plough, it was left in Mr. Worby's hands to put into practical form. The result of this was the *de facto* solution of the problem, for from the day of the first trial of the balance plough progress was rapid and easy. Fortunately we have preserved a photograph of the actual first balance plough made, the inscription upon which vouches for the date, and is as follows : " Photograph of the first Steam Plough made for J. Fowler at Messrs. Ransomes and Sims' Orwell Works, Ipswich, constructed by William Worby, and first put to work, April 10th, 1856, on a farm at Nacton, the property of Sir George Brook, and in the occupation of Mr. Farrar." Signed " Wm. Worby."

" Very soon after the success achieved by this plough improvements were introduced for facilitating the steering of the implement, and also for lengthening and shortening the rope for fields with irregular boundaries, and also for managing the slack of the rope. In fact the plough had, essentially, arrived at its present well known form when Mr. Fowler established his Steam Plough Works at Leeds.

" There was of course an immense amount of collateral scheming and experimental work in adapting an engine for the purpose of drawing the plough over the land. This was only partially successful until the invention of the celebrated *clip drum* (invented by Mr. Burton) removed the last difficulty in this branch of the business. Another important adjunct contributing much to the success of steam ploughing as a whole, was the travelling anchor, which travelled forwards along the headland at the same rate as the engine on the opposite side of the field. This was patented in 1856."

The exhibition of Mr. Fowler's steam draining apparatus at Lincoln in 1854 is considered the point from which the practical history of the cultivation of the land by steam may be dated. It was there that the practical mind of Mr. Smith, of Woolston, suggested its wider application, and fresh experiments began to be made.

The success which crowned Mr. Fowler's persevering efforts came slowly and by degrees. Experiment followed experiment, and improvements continued to be made till in July, 1864, he achieved a sort of final triumph by his exhibition of two engines of 7-horse power, working simultaneously on opposite headlands. The expedition with which these engines were set down and completed their work was a matter of admiration to all present, and secured high compliments from the judges.

The anxious thought and close application to business which these pursuits involved told unfavourably upon Mr. Fowler's health, and in the autumn of this year he occasionally sought relaxation and exercise in the hunting field. On one of these occasions, in the middle of November, he was unfortunately thrown from his horse and sustained a compound fracture of his arm. Serious complications arose, and death resulted at Acworth, near Pontefract, on December 4th, 1864. A wife and five children were left to mourn this heavy loss. The life which thus closed at the early age of 38 years was one in which not only much important work was done, but many estimable qualities manifested, and hosts of friends gained. In all his varied relations in life Mr. Fowler was highly esteemed. He felt a kindly interest in the welfare of his work-people, and was beloved by them in return. By his coadjutors in his special pursuits he was held in much personal regard. Many are the testimonies borne to his excellence of heart and life. "I would willingly do what lies in my power," says Mr. Byng, "to perpetuate the memory of one with whom it was so pleasant to be occupied as the late Mr. John Fowler."

Mr. Fowler was a well-made and handsome man, with a prepossessing countenance of intelligent and kindly expression. Both his character and person justify Mr. E. Ruck's remark that "all who knew him looked on him as a pattern of a thorough Englishman."

We may fitly close this brief sketch with a condensed notice of the introduction of steam ploughing to the Continent. On the 31st of March, 1868, the steam plough made its triumphal entry into France. It had been previously exhibited at the great Paris Exhibition, and on the day mentioned upwards of 10,000 farmers assembled on the Plains of Berry to witness the inauguration of steam ploughing. One of John Fowler's ploughs accomplished its work to the admiration of the beholders, and received the benediction of the Bishop of Bourges. A grand banquet followed, at which it was announced that the Emperor Louis Napoleon had awarded a gold medal to the French firm who had purchased and introduced the plough, and among other toasts was one to the memory of the Wiltshire inventor, John Fowler.

About two miles south of Box Station, and seven miles west of Melksham, is the small village of *Monkton Farley*. A monastery of Cluniac monks once stood here, and flourished under the patronage and benefactions of the Empress Maud, Henry III., and others. It was suppressed at the Reformation, and the building either then or subsequently destroyed. Some interesting tombs have been discovered on the site, and from the few architectural fragments which remain it is conjectured that the church must have been a beautiful structure. To many minds, however, the chief interest with which this village is invested arises from the fact that it was the death place of the excellent Dr. John Jewel, Bishop of Salisbury. This eminent prelate, "the wonder of his age for his knowledge in divinity, and a most strenuous defender of the reformed religion," was also a frequent and zealous preacher, and spent much of his time in travelling about his diocese and overseeing his clergy. It was while so employed that death overtook him. On Saturday, Sept. 16, 1571, he was on his way to preach at Lacock, when he was met by a gentleman who, seeing that he was ill, strongly advised him to go back. Declining this kind and prudent advice, the Bishop, with more zeal than wisdom, pursued his journey, and with painful effort preached from the words, "Walk in the Spirit." It was his last sermon. His symptoms grew worse, and on the following Saturday he died at Monkton Farley, whence his body was removed for burial in Salisbury Cathedral.

" There are few towns in Wiltshire more interesting to the archæologist or the student of Natural History than *Bradford-upon-Avon*." The correctness of this remark, with which the Rev. W. H. Jones, M.A., vicar of the parish, commences a series of papers in *The Wiltshire Magazine*, is confirmed by the facts he presents in his History of this picturesque locality. The closing pages of this account are devoted to " Old Families and Worthies." Here we meet with the Halls, the Rogers's, the Yerburys, and the Methuens. We also find that General Shrapnell, who for the invention of the terribly destructive projectile which bears his name, was rewarded with a pension of £1200 a year, was a native of this town, where he also died in 1842 ; and was buried in the parish church. Here, too, General Bush, an officer who served with great distinction in the West Indies, was born. He died in 1854. The Rev.

HENRY HARVEY,

who, though not a native, was, as Vicar of the parish, a resident for seventeen years, deservedly finds a place among its Worthies. During his incumbency he "accomplished," says Mr. Jones, " a great work for the parish at large—a work more lasting in its benefits than had before been completed since the Reformation." One church was built ; two were rebuilt and enlarged ; and three more or less improved and restored ; the vicarage house was rebuilt, and a new parsonage provided for the District Church. Mr. Harvey removed to Olveston in Gloucestershire, in 1850, where he died in 1854.

To this list other worthy names can be added.

Dr. Winter Hamilton, urging some friends who were writing the biography of a recently deceased minister to do their work quickly, used as a reason that " ministers are soon forgotten." This witness is true, especially with reference to preachers in large cities. It is, however, a rule with exceptions ; and in a limited and somewhat select circle of London Congregationalists, the Rev.

JAMES STRATTEN

is probably one. This eminent preacher was born at Bradford-on-Avon, on May 26th, 1795. At an early age he was remarkable for his intelligence, aptitude for learning, and deep religious thoughtfulness. The family removing to Holt, James, while quite a youth, became a member of the

Independent Church at Trowbridge. An incident occurred about this time which he afterwards thus related:—"One day, in the month of January last, I went on business to the house of the Rev. Edward Spencer, a pious and Evangelical clergyman. After my business was settled, conversation turned upon religious topics, in course of which he asked me if ever I had any thoughts of the ministry. I could not deny but I had. He then said he should be glad to see my father on the subject, who accordingly a few days afterwards went to his house. Mr. Spencer then proposed to take me to his own house for a year and a half or two years, and then send me to Oxford free of every expense, which proposal, after serious deliberation and earnest prayer, and having asked the advice of my religious friends, who were desirous of leaving me to my own choice, I declined, because I could not conscientiously conform to the discipline of the Established Church." At the age of seventeen he entered Hoxton Academy, and after a four years' course of study, went to Dublin, where he preached for two years. He then returned to London : became minister of Paddington Chapel; married the eldest daughter of the excellent Mr. Thomas Wilson, and soon found himself the centre of an overflowing congregation, comprising many of the *elite* of metropolitan nonconformity. His preaching, while not remarkable for originality or depth of thought, was singularly interesting. His thoughts, which were lucidly expressed, were often accompanied by striking illustrations : while thoughtfulness, elegance and tenderness were invariable characteristics of his discourses. To his moral influence high testimony has been borne. One who knew him well said " he was very distinctly a power for godliness in a very wide circle." Overtures came to him from the Church of England to accept lucrative positions in the Establishment, but these were declined. For upwards of forty years Mr. Stratten maintained his popularity, and when through failing strength, he retired from his pastorate, it was amidst the regrets of his congregation. He was an intimate friend of Mr. Jay, and between the characters and careers of these fellow county men, there were points of interesting resemblance. During the last years of his life he published a volume of sermons, under the title of *Freedom and Happiness in Christ.* This was followed by a smaller volume, containing, among other discourses, one on the "Intermediate

State," a thoughtful and earnest effort to look "behind the veil." Sustained, amidst the infirmities of age, by the hope of a glorious immortality, he passed "behind the veil," May 12, 1872.

RICHARD LUTTRELL PILKINGTON BETHELL, LORD WESTBURY,

the son of a physician, was born at Bradford, June 30th, 1800. He received his early education at Bristol, where he made such remarkable progress that at the age of little more than fourteen, and while still wearing a jacket and a frill, he went to Wadham College, Oxford, for matriculation. In a few months he had gained a scholarship, and in his 18th year took his Bachelor's degree. He remained at Oxford for some time "coaching," till being entered a student at the Middle Temple, he was called to the bar in 1823. Settling in London he assiduously applied himself to the study of his profession, and selected the Chancery Bar for the scene of his practice. At the age of twenty-five he married, thus throwing up a fellowship he held in his own college, but finding a good wife in Elinor Mary, daughter of Mr. Robert Abraham. His professional success was extraordinary, and for more than twenty years he was engaged in nearly every important Chancery suit of that period. In 1847 he sought Parliamentary honours as a Liberal-Conservative by contesting Shaftesbury, but was defeated. Four years afterwards he was returned as a Liberal for Aylesbury, and in 1852 took office as Solicitor-General under the Government of the Earl of Aberdeen, receiving at the same time the honour of knighthood. In 1856 he became Attorney-General. While holding these offices he introduced several important measures of Law Reform. Withdrawing from Aylesbury in 1859, he was immediately elected for the important borough of Wolverhampton.

About this period the Rev. W. H. Jones made the following graceful reference to Sir Richard: "Our business as archæologists is not with the living but with the dead; otherwise we might dwell proudly on the successful course of that distinguished native of Bradford-on-Avon, Her Majesty's late Attorney-General, Sir Richard Bethell, in whose high position his fellow-townsmen recognise no less the acknowledgment of eminent talents, than the reward of untiring perseverance." An old Greek proverb warns us to "Call no man happy till he is dead," and an English one of like import says, "Praise a fair day at night." Events in the subsequent career of this eminent lawyer justify the almost ungenerous caution which these proverbs suggest.

On the death of Lord Campbell, in 1861, the Seals were offered to Sir Richard Bethell, and as Lord Westbury, of Westbury, in his native county, he took his seat on the woolsack. He had probably reached the height of his ambition, and he filled his office with consummate ability. "On the woolsack," says the *Times*, "and in the Equity Courts, during his three years' tenure of the Great Seal, Lord Westbury made his mark, and there are few of his predecessors in the present century whose judgments can be said to stand higher. His great merits, both as an advocate and as a Judge, were ease and self-possession, clearness of thought, exquisite precision, and conciseness of language, and a marvellously acute logical faculty, with a mind capable at once of entertaining the broadest views and the most subtle distinctions." The sun that thus shone so brightly was doomed to go down with dimmed splendour. We need not, as the authority already quoted generously said, "re-open the melancholy question of Lord Westbury's fall. It will be enough to say that in the summer of 1865 scandals which, though not originating with him, it was felt he ought to have detected and checked, were brought to light in connection with the Leeds Bankruptcy Court, and in consequence of these, and of an adverse motion proposed in the House of Commons, he resigned the Great Seal in July of that year." His act of resignation in the House of Lords was so singularly dignified and manly that Mr. Molesworth says "it was generally felt that nothing he had done in his office, and he had effected much, better became him than his manner of leaving it."

As one of the "Law Lords" Lord Westbury continued to take part in the business of the House of Peers till within a short period of his death, which took place on Sunday, July 21st, 1873, the day following the sudden death of Bishop Wilberforce.

The beautiful old mansion known as "Kingston House," is one of the chief architectural features of Bradford. It was built by one of the Halls in the reign of James I. About the middle of last century it was the property and residence of the Duke of Kingston. The notoriety of the lady whom he married was unenviably great. The Duchess's whole life was one of "adventure, display, and indelicate publicity." Traditional tales of her peculiarities still linger in Bradford, but are not worth recording.

Three miles south-east of Bradford is the ancient cloth manufacturing town of *Trowbridge*. "The towne," says Leland writing in the reign of Henry VIII., "standeth on a rokky hill, and is very welle buildyd of stone, and florisheth by Drapery." Its history has many points of interest, and contains some names which are entitled to a place in our list.

SAMUEL BREWER,

a native of this town, where he had an estate and was engaged in the woollen manufacture, was a botanist of some note. After accompanying Dillins in his botanical excursions in 1726, he remained some time in Wales collecting the Cryptogamia. In 1728 he removed to Bradford in Yorkshire, where he employed himself in a work to be entitled *The Botanical Guide*, but it was never printed.

GEORGE KEATE,

a descendant of the ancient families of Seymour and Hungerford, who was born here in 1730, has acquired some celebrity, as a poet and miscellaneous writer. He was sent to school at Kingston-upon-Thames; after which he spent some years at Geneva, where he formed an intimacy with Voltaire. Returning to England, he was articled to an attorney, and in due course called to the bar. His hopes of success and honour in his profession were not realised; and he accordingly devoted himself to the more congenial pursuits of literature. His pen was facile; and his works in prose and verse are varied and numerous. Among others he wrote *Ancient and Modern Rome, a Poem written at Rome 1755; The History of Geneva; An Epistle from Lady Jane Grey to Lord Guildford Dudley*, in verse; *Netley Abbey*, an elegiac poem; and *Ferney*, an epistle to Voltaire. In this last named work he paid a high tribute to the genius of Shakespeare, which was so warmly appreciated by the authorities of Stratford-on-Avon, that they presented him with a silver mounted standish, made of the wood of the famous mulberry tree planted by the great dramatist. This probably encouraged him to attempt a dramatic poem himself, and he wrote *The Monuments of Arcadia*, in 1773. He published a collection of his poetical works in two volumes, in 1781.

Mr. Keate appears to have been not only a man of talent and taste, but of amiable and excellent disposition and character. The profits of his last and most popular work, *An Account of the Pelew Islands*, compiled from the records of Captain Wilson, and published in 1788, were devoted to benevolent purposes. He died June 27, 1797. The birthplace of one poet, Trowbridge has been also the residence of another, whose name is more widely known and whose fame will be more lasting than that of her own native son. For eighteen years the Rev.

GEORGE CRABBE

was rector of this parish, where the evening of his life was spent in the peaceful discharge of his clerical duties. His literary work had been accomplished and his fame won long before he became a resident in Wiltshire. It is, however, interesting to note his acknowledged obligations to two distinguished members of a great Wiltshire family. In his Preface to an edition of his works published in 1807, he tells of his introduction, at the seat of Mr. Burke, to the Hon. Charles James Fox ; and gratefully relates how in after years the statesman, "engaged by the affairs of a great empire, and struggling with the inveteracy of a fatal disease," yet afforded him the benefit of his criticism. "Nor can I," he says, "deny myself the melancholy satisfaction of adding that *The Parish Register* (and more especially the story of *Phœbe Dawson*, with some parts of the second book,) were the last compositions of their kind, that amused the capacious, the candid, the benevolent mind of this great Man." This collection of his poems is dedicated to Mr. Fox's nephew, the late well-known Lord Holland, from whom the poet had received many expressions of kindly regard.

Mr. Crabbe was presented with the living of Trowbridge by the Duke of

Rutland in 1813, being then nearly sixty years of age, and he here found a happy home and spent a serene old age. In addition to the pleasures he derived from numerous friendships, he found delightful recreation in his favourite pursuits—botany and geology; and was often seen in the woods and fields, or hammer in hand, fossil hunting in the quarries of the locality. It was during his residence here that his brother poets—Rogers and Moore—effected for him the sale of the copyright of his works, for which they obtained the sum of £3000 from Mr. Murray. In connection with this transaction Moore tells the following anecdote as illustrating, not only Crabbe's satisfaction with the arrangement, but also the simplicity of his character:—"When he received the bills for £3000 we earnestly advised that he should without delay deposit them in some safe hands ; but no, he must 'take them with him to Trowbridge and show them to his son John. They would hardly believe in his good luck at home if they did not see the bills.' On his way down to Trowbridge a friend at Salisbury (Mr. Everett, the banker), at whose house he rested, seeing that he carried these bills loosely in his waistcoat pocket, requested to be allowed to take charge of them for him ; but with equal ill-success. 'There was no fear,' he said, 'of his losing them, and he must show them to his son John.'" He died on Feb. 3, 1832, at the age of 78, and is buried in his own church, where his parishioners have erected a monument to the memory of their revered pastor, whose name cannot fail to live as that of

"Nature's sternest painter, and her best."

Two nonconformist ministers of this town, belonging to two widely different sections of the Christian Church, have left names which are likely to be long remembered by their friends and admirers.

As a minister of the small sect of Particular Baptists,

JOHN WARBURTON

for many years exercised great influence among his fellow religionists in Trowbridge and other parts of Wiltshire. A man of original character and some native talent, there is much in the narrative of his life interesting to others besides those of his own denomination. "I was born at Stand," he says, "about five miles from Manchester, in October, 1776. My parents being poor, I had but little opportunity of acquiring human learning, though, by the tender mercy of God, I obtained a little reading and writing, a blessing for which I have often felt thankful." " *The Mercies of a Covenant God,*" a sort of autobiographical narrative, which he first published in 1834, abounds with records of strange experiences. He was brought up as a weaver, married early, and for some years "was given up to all manner of wickedness." Drunkenness seems to have been his chief besetment, and public houses were his delight. At length, strangely arrested in this evil course, he became a member of an Independent Church, but afterwards joined the Baptists. Encouraged by his friends, he began to preach, and soon became popular.

A little company meeting in a room at Bury, in Lancashire, engaged his services at four shillings a week for twelve months! This continued till one of the deacons reproachfully asked him how he "could have a good conscience in taking four shillings a week from such a few poor people." About 1810 he removed to Rochdale as minister of a new congregation. Here his salary was twenty-five shillings per week. A Chapel was built, and for a time he struggled on ; "but," he says, "I soon got up to the neck in trouble." With a family of eight children, a troublesome deacon, and " over head and years in debt," the perplexed preacher felt that the time had come for removal. He was invited to "preach on trial" at Maidstone, and a day or two afterwards he received, he says, "a letter from a few people who met in a room at Trowbridge, in Wiltshire, inviting me for a month on trial, if I was at liberty." At Maidstone he found "everything as pleasant to flesh and blood" as he could desire ; but "could see nothing but difficulties, trials, and miseries at Trowbridge." To Trowbridge, however, he came in 1812. The "few people" increased, and in 1816 the room was left, and Zion Chapel was opened. Here Mr. Warburton continued to preach till his death, April 2, 1857, in his eighty-first year.

His life, as described by himself, in a phraseology peculiar to his denomination, was an almost incessant struggle ; and his sermons as well as his writings were largely seasoned with details of these experiences.

Spiritual "ins and outs, roarings and rejoicings," struggles with poverty, temptations to self-destruction, unvarnished confessions of inward evil, strange dreams, remarkable helps and wonderful deliverances, were freely related to illustrate and confirm the dogmas he taught. He did little to supplement the deficiencies of his early education, and held human learning in light esteem. His pronunciation was broad, and his manner in the pulpit entirely unconventional. Yet, even men of culture listened occasionally to his preaching with deep attention, and were moved to tears by his quaint pathos. One instance of this occurred at Cirencester, when he was preaching at the opening of a new chapel in 1854. His head was covered with a red cotton pocket handkerchief, and he otherwise presented such an appearance as to excite a general smile. His sermon, however, was one of singular impressiveness. The harsh dogmas of his creed were relieved by striking original illustrations, and those whose minds had but little sympathy with his doctrinal opinions wept as they listened to his pathetic narrations. In one of these he told, with much minuteness and graphic power, how he had once solemnly vowed to send the first sovereign he should receive to his "poor old mother." That very morning a sovereign unexpectedly came, and with it came the temptation to have a pipe and think the matter over. A process of reasoning, which he carefully described, led him to think he would send only fifteen shillings instead of the full amount. Still whiffing and reasoning, he next satisfied himself that it would be right to divide the pound, keeping half for himself and sending half-a-sovereign to his mother. At length he arrived at the conclusion that his mother would be very thankful for even five shillings, and that, therefore, he would send her that sum. "Suddenly," he said, "I saw that this was all a temptation of the devil, and I put down my pipe in such a hurry that I brauk un. So I writ a letter, put the sovereign inside, and hurrying to the Post Office, I put the letter in, and said, 'There, Mr. Devil, thee bee'st done.'" This was but a specimen of his usual style, and it was therefore no wonder that among those of his own peculiar opinions he should have been popular and influential.

A residence of more than half a century in the town of Trowbridge, a character of highest excellence, and a life of active self-denying Christian labours, entitle the Rev.

SAMUEL MARTIN,

for fifty years the faithful and beloved minister of Conigree General Baptist (or Unitarian) Chapel, to a place among the worthies of Wiltshire. Mr. Martin was born at Nantwich, in Cheshire, October 16, 1801. His early education was chiefly conducted by his father, who belonged to an old Scotch family, and who, having suffered some reverses of fortune, at that time kept a private school. Samuel was apprenticed to a wholesale ironmonger, and so highly satisfied was his master with his abilities and conduct, that on the expiration of his apprenticeship he proposed to take him as a partner. This offer the young man declined, having set his heart on becoming a minister. For some time his mind had been exercised with religious subjects. Although his father and family usually attended either the Presbyterian Chapel or the Established Church, Samuel frequently worshipped with the Wesleyans. About this time he resolved to be baptised, and as there was no Baptist Chapel in Nantwich he set out and walked to Rawtenstall, where he was baptised by a Mr. Ingram. He soon afterwards began to preach, his first sermon being delivered at the Independent Chapel in his native town. In these movements he appears to have acted with much independence of thought, and with great freedom from sectarian prejudices and restraints. The Rev. Richard Wright, then minister of Conigree Chapel, happening to visit Nantwich, met with Mr. Martin and engaged him in some missionary operations in Cornwall. Here he remained till 1826, when he became Minister of the Unitarian Chapel at Marshfield, in Gloucestershire. In 1827 he was invited to Trowbridge as the successor of Mr. Wright, and chiefly through the influence of a clergyman he accepted the invitation. The story is so singular and good that we give it as told by himself. He was engaged to preach at Trowbridge by special invitation, and says, "On the Saturday evening I stood at the bottom of the street at Bath to wait for the Trowbridge coach. It came up quite full outside, so I was obliged to get inside, and there in one corner of the coach sat an old clergyman, whom I afterwards discovered to be the Rev. Mr. Bryce, rector of Porlock. We had much interesting conversation, in the course of which he learnt that Trowbridge was to be my probable destination, and that I was to preach there the next day with a view to my settlement as minister. The old gentleman and I parted company in the Market-place, and he went to visit my friend Miss Waldron. There was at that time no service in the chapel on Sunday mornings, as Mr. Wright was accustomed to preach at Bradford. But in the afternoon when I entered the pulpit, I saw, to my utter amazement, the old clergyman sitting right before me in Mr. Waldron's pew. I looked at him, and heartily wished him out of the chapel. I felt very nervous and uncomfortable during the service, and after it was over, I kept my seat in the pulpit for a long time, determined not to go down till the old gentleman was gone; for I felt he would severely criticise the many mistakes that I knew I had made. When he was gone, I went down into the vestry, and determined, after due consideration, that I would give up all thought of settling here, feeling that it was such a 'dead-alive' place. I determined to go away by the early coach next morning, in order to avoid meeting the old clergyman, whom I hoped never to see again. That I might be sure of not seeing him, I kept out of the town, and crossed the Innox fields, in order to get into the coach as it passed. When it came up it was quite full outside. I was obliged to go inside; and when I opened the coach door, there, to my consternation, sat the old gentleman whom I had taken such pains to avoid. He welcomed me most kindly, encouraged me, and at length said, ' You *will* settle at Trowbridge ?' But I answered ' No,' and gave him my various reasons. He said earnestly and almost prophetically, ' God has a work for you to do at Trowbridge—go. I will not leave you until you give me your promise that you will.' The promise was at length given. I came here, and until the day of his death the old gentleman was one of my most faithful friends. His heart was open, and at his house there was always a home for me."

Mr. Martin's work at Trowbridge was attended by much success. The congregation greatly increased, the chapel was improved, and the whole state of things grew stronger and brighter. In January 1829, the young minister married Miss Odgers, of Flushing, Cornwall, who for seventeen years was "a help meet for him" in home and church. She died in 1846, at the age of 38, leaving a son and four daughters to mourn her departure. His second wife was the widow of Mr. Henry Whitefield.

To supplement his slender income Mr. Martin commenced a day school for boys in 1842, which he carried on for twelve years, thus making a heavy addition to the labours of his active and self-denying life. In 1857 the old chapel being in a decayed and dangerous condition was taken down and the present handsome building erected. Commodious schoolrooms were built in 1865. These changes and improvements were accomplished chiefly through the earnest efforts of Mr. Martin. Incessant labour told upon a frame not robust, and in June, 1872, Mr. Martin was struck down by a fit of apoplexy. From this attack he so far recovered as to be able to preach occasionally till within about two years of his death, which occurred July 27, 1877. This event was sincerely and generally mourned. Mr. Martin's influence had been great and good; and his relations with men of all religious parties had been cordial. He had enjoyed the friendship of the poet Crabbe, and other clergymen of the town and neighbourhood; as well as that of dissenters of all denominations. A long procession of mourners of all classes and opinions followed his bier to the grave.

Canon Jackson referring to eminent natives of *Steeple Ashton* tells a droll story of "an eminent sheep-stealer." "I found the story," he says, "among old John Aubrey's papers, in a cupboard at Oxford, in a letter written from London, by one John Hoskins, serjeant-at-law, to Aubrey, which runs thus :—

London, December 14, 1661.

Mr. AUBREY,—I have bin told that in the time of Baron Tanfield, about 1620, there was indicted one John Brewer, of Stiple Ashton, for sheep-stealing, who had a trick to keep the mutton sweet seven weeks without salt, but would not tell his way to the Judge, no not at his trial. He was acquitted. Now will you oblige me and some other of your servants, if you can enquire how this was done.—Your servant,

JOHN HOSKINS.

Aubrey was not in the secret, but probably being as anxious to obtain it as the London lawyer was, he immediately wrote to Mr. Robert Beach, of Steeple Ashton, seeking the desired information. The reply, which if not quite satisfactory, was brief and conclusive, ran thus:—

The manner is this: Near Claverton, by Bath, in the stone quarries, are some caves; and this Brewer, the sheep-stealer, kept his stolen sheep in the caves *alive!* This was the *secret.*

"The autobiography and correspondence of

MARY GRANVILLE,—MRS. DELANY :

with interesting reminiscences of King George the Third and Queen Charlotte," edited by the Right Hon. Lady Llanover, and published in three volumes, in 1861, is an elaborate memoir of an eminent Wiltshire lady.

"I was born," she says, "in the year 1700, at a small country house of my father's at *Coulston,* in Wiltshire. My father was grandson of Sir Bevil Granville, who was killed on Lansdown, in the year 1648, fighting for his king and country. A monument was erected on the spot, recording his loyalty, his valour, and his death. Bernard, my grandfather, youngest son of Sir Bevil, was the messenger to Charles II. of the joyful tidings that he might return to his Kingdom in safety. My uncle George was created Lord Lansdown by Queen Anne, and my father Bernard married a daughter of Sir Martin Westcomb."

When about seventeen, Miss Granville spent some time with her uncle at Bowood, where her marriage to a Mr. Pendarves—a Cornish gentleman, forty-three years older than herself—was arranged. She submitted to her "unhappy fortune," fulfilling for seven weary years the duties of a wife to a man whom she should never have accepted as a husband. After a widowhood of nineteen years, during which she had several offers of marriage, she became the wife of Dr. Patrick Delany, and it is as Mrs. Delany she has become known to posterity. In many respects she was a remarkable woman. She was eminently skilled in painting and embroidery;

and possessed poetical talents of no mean order. Her circle of friends and admirers was large, and included several of distinguished rank and talent ; among the most intimate were Earl Bathurst and Dean Swift, with the latter of whom she kept up a regular correspondence for some years. At the age of eighty-three she became blind, but this affliction neither affected the amiability of her temper, nor the cheerfulness of her mind. She died in 1788, the day after completing her eighty-eighth year. There is a fine portrait of her in Hampton Court.

The great battle—commonly called the battle of Ethandun—in which Alfred, after his temporary concealment at Athelney, so decisively defeated the Danes, is supposed to have been fought in the neighbourhood of *Edington*, some four miles north-east of Westbury.

WILLIAM DE EDINGTON,

as his name implies, belonged to this parish, where he was born about 1300. He was educated at Oxford, and after holding several livings in different counties he was preferred to the See of Winchester. Being a favourite with Edward III., on account of his great political talents, he was also appointed Lord High Treasurer of England. Some parts of his conduct in this latter office appear to have been of very questionable character ; but he gave such satisfaction to the King that when the Order of the Garter was instituted Edington was made King's Prelate, or Chancellor of the Order, which honour was to descend to his successors in the bishopric. It is more satisfactory to see him turning his thoughts to the spiritual wants of his native village, where he built a monastic church and instituted a fraternity of monks called *Bonhommes*. They belonged to the Order of St. Augustine, but were of a particular class which was selected by the Bishop at the suggestion of the Black Prince. In 1357 he was promoted to the high office of Lord Chancellor of England, and in 1366 was elected Archbishop of Canterbury. He is said to have declined this latter honour from motives of avarice, remarking, in appropriate *stall* phraseology, " Though Canterbury is the higher rack, yet Winchester is the richer manger." Advanced age and infirmities might have been the true reason, for we find that he died towards the end of the same year. He was buried in the Cathedral, the nave of which he had begun to rebuild, and for the completion of which great work he left a considerable sum of money.

The name of another ecclesiastic,

WILLIAM AISCOUGH,

Bishop of Salisbury, is tragically associated with this quiet village. This prelate, who had stood high in the favour of the gentle but weak Henry VI., was made Bishop in 1438, and on the occasion of his consecration in Windsor Chapel the King appointed him his confessor. Some state offices were also held by him, and probably in the discharge of these he became an object of popular suspicion and dislike. From some motives, perhaps the highest and the best, he appears to have resigned these more worldly appointments, and resolved to devote himself, at least for a season, to religious exercises in his own palace at Edington. Here he might well have hoped for peace. But a storm which had gathered in Kent was extending to other parts of the land. The discontents of the oppressed people, fomented by John Mortimer *alias* Jack Cade, were finding vent in ignorant and savage outrages. The wild spirit of insurrection reached Wiltshire, and a mob consisting chiefly of the Bishop's own tenants marked him for a victim. What their particular grievances were we are not told, but their vengeance was deadly. On June 29th, 1450, they entered his palace, and rushing to the church found him ministering at the altar. With fierce cries they dragged him forth and hurrying him to the adjacent hill-top stoned him to death. Leaving the mangled corpse stripped of the episcopal vestments and covered with blood, the murderers returned to the palace, which they spoiled of 10,000 marks—an immense sum which the unfortunate prelate had by some means accumulated. The Lord Say, one of Henry's most unpopular ministers, who perished in the same insurrection, is represented by Shakespeare as expostulating with Cade :—

> Unless you be possessed with devilish spirits,
> You cannot but forbear to murder me.

And then earnestly pleading for his life :—

> Tell me wherein have I offended most?
> Have I affected wealth or honour? speak.
> Are my chests filled with extorted gold?
> Is my apparel sumptuous to behold?
> Whom have I injured that ye seek my death?
> These hands are free from guiltless blood shedding.
> This heart from harbouring foul deceitful thoughts.
> O let me live!

Whether the Bishop could have used such pleas for life, or whether he stood self-condemned and speechless, it is not for us to judge; guilty or innocent he suffered a cruel death.

PART II.

WEST WILTS.—*SOUTH.*

"Cast down thyself, and only strive to raise
The glory of thy Maker's sacred name;
Use all thy powers, that blessed power to praise
Which gives thee power to be, and use the same."

SIR JOHN DAVIES.

"Almost every memento of celebrated personages is desired and welcomed, and readers are anxious and eager to catch at every trifling anecdote that helps to form a conception of their individuality, or to connect their private history with their public fame."

WILLIAM JAY.

 ASSING from Edington to Bratton we enter the South Division of the County, and soon reach Westbury, at the base of Bratton Hill, on the side of which figures the great White Horse, said to commemorate the victory of Alfred over the Danes. With this ancient parliamentary borough we connect several eminent names.

BRYAN EDWARDS,

a merchant and author of considerable repute, was born here May 21st, 1743. He was educated in Bristol, and afterwards spent many years in Jamaica, where he inherited great property from an uncle. On his return to England he attracted much attention by his writings on West Indian affairs. He became a member of Parliament for Grampound in Cornwall, and died in 1800. His contemporaries deemed him a man of high ability.

DR. PHILIP WITHERS,

a clergyman, and a writer of considerable distinction, was also a native of Westbury, where he was born about the middle of last century. His father was a blue dyer, and Philip was apprenticed to a country shopkeeper. It was not till he was in his twentieth year that he acquired even the rudiments of education. After some time he went to Queen's College, Cambridge, and attained unusual proficiency in the Greek and Latin languages. On leaving college, Dr. Withers opened an academy in London, and also obtained the lectureship at St. Clements, Eastcheap. He now commenced his literary career by writing powerful pamphlets, chiefly on political subjects. Some of these gave great offence to the Prince of Wales, and Withers was prosecuted in the Court of King's Bench. He was sentenced to twelve months' imprisonment in Newgate. While undergoing this punishment he overheated himself in a game of fives, and falling into a fever, died July, 1790.

With the history of modern Christian missions, and with each other, the names of Carey, Marshman, and Ward are closely associated as those of three early and most devoted fellow missionaries in India. Wiltshire can claim one of this noble trio, Westbury Leigh having been the birthplace of

DR. JOSHUA MARSHMAN,

who was born April 20th, 1768. On the side of his father, who was a weaver, he traced his descent from an officer in Cromwell's army, and on that of his mother from a family of French Protestant refugees. Both parents were members of the Baptist Church, at Westbury Leigh, of which his father was also a deacon. His early education at the village school furnished him with nothing more than a knowledge of reading. Beyond this he received no scholastic training, and at an early age began to follow the craft of his father. His efforts at self education were earnest and persistent, and his thirst for knowledge made him an insatiable reader. He borrowed books of all kinds, read them with avidity and filled his mind with a strange medley of history, geography, science, poetry and religion. When about fifteen he spent a short time in London as shop boy in the employ of a bookseller. Here he found opportunities for reading of which he eagerly availed himself. "But the labour of trudging through the streets, day after day, with a heavy parcel of books, became at length disheartening, and having been one day sent to the Duke of Grafton with three folio volumes of Clarendon's History, he began to give way to melancholy, and as he passed Westminster Abbey, laid down the load, and sobbed at the thought that there was no higher prospect before him in life than that of a bookseller's porter; but looking up at the building, and recalling to mind the noble associations connected with it, he brushed away his tears, replaced the load on his shoulders, and walked on with a light heart, determined to bide his time." His father recalled him to Westbury, and he resumed his labours at the loom, together with his old habit of desultory reading. Before he was eighteen he had read more than five hundred volumes. Some special subjects, however, now engaged his attention. As he plied the shuttle he studied the Greek grammar and cultivated those gifts which in after years rendered him distinguished as a linguist. His mind also felt the power of religious influences and he gave earnest attention to divinity.

At the age of twenty-three Mr. Marshman married Hannah Shepherd, granddaughter of an aged Baptist minister at Crockerton; and three years afterwards was appointed master of a school connected with the Baptist Church at Broadmead, Bristol. Of this Church he became a member. Favoured with the friendship of Dr. Ryland, President of the Baptist Academy, he was permitted to join the classes of that institution; and for five years devoted his leisure hours to the study of the classics, together with that of Hebrew and Syriac. Becoming deeply interested in the missionary enterprise in India, he offered his services to the committee of the Baptist Society; and with Mr. Ward, of Derby, sailed for Calcutta. At Serampore they were joined by Dr. Carey, and commenced those united labours which have rendered their associated names memorable in the annals of Christian missions. What these labours were cannot be fully told. Mr. Marshman's great energies were fully thrown into the work, and his self-denying toils were incessant. By severe application he acquired an intimate knowledge of the Bengalee, Sanskrit, and Chinese languages. These attainments he used in translations of the Gospels and other parts of the New Testament into Chinese; in the preparation of grammars; and also in valuable assistance rendered to Dr. Carey in Sanskrit and Bengali works. Travelling, preaching, teaching, printing; amidst dangers, diffi-

E

culties, and opposition ; exercising self-denial and sacrificing health, he and his colleagues pursued their course with apostolic zeal. It is humiliating to think of Sydney Smith abusing his splendid powers by denouncing these noble men as "consecrated coblers," "low-born and low-bred mechanics ;" and their great work as "a perilous heap of trash." The only excuse for him is that of ignorance : he knew not what he did ; but he ought to have known. It is satisfactory to learn that he lived to see and regret his error.

Mr. Marshman's literary acquirements and labours were acknowledged by Brown University in the United States, which in 1811 honoured him with the diploma of Doctor of Divinity. It is worthy of note that the first Eastern newspaper ever published was originated by Dr. Marshman and fellow workers. It was called *The Mirror of News* and was printed in the native language. The first number appeared May 31st, 1818. It soon grew popular, and Lord Hastings being of opinion that such a paper must be "extensively and importantly useful," allowed it to pass through the post at one fourth the usual rate.

In 1826 Dr. Marshman visited England. Landing at Brighton he posted down to Wiltshire. "In his diary," says his son, "he describes the ecstacy of his feelings as he gazed on the old white horse chalked out on the slope of the hill near Westbury, and drove through the scenes of his boyhood, and traversed the streets in which every spot called up some cherished recollection. He reached his native village on Sunday morning, and entered the old meeting-house, where he joined some of his old friends, and the sons and grandsons of others, at the communion table. He passed three days in visiting the few companions of his youth who still survived, and was delighted to find himself again addressed by the familiar name of Joshua." After some stay in England he went to Copenhagen and obtained from the King of Denmark a charter for the College at Serampore which was at that time a Danish possession. He next visited Germany, France, Scotland and Ireland. Everywhere he was received with expressions of highest respect, and introduced to many distinguished men.

Returning to India he resumed his work, which he continued notwithstanding failing health and painful bereavements till his death in 1837.

Of Dr. Marshman's numerous family only six survived him. His eldest son, in *The Story of Carey, Marshman, and Ward, the Serampore Missionaries*, has given an admirable "record of his labours and his virtues," from which the foregoing particulars have been obtained. His youngest daughter became Lady Havelock—wife of Sir Henry Havelock, of Indian fame.

Campanologists may be interested to know that the largest bell in Wiltshire is the tenor of Westbury belfry. It is 58 inches in diameter and weighs 85 cwt. It was cast, as were many others in the county, by Rudhall, of Gloucester.

Still moving Southward we reach *Warminster*, pleasantly lying at a western extremity of Salisbury Plain, and visited by the Wiley, as it comes down from the Deverill valley. This ancient town was the birthplace of

DR. SAMUEL SQUIRE,

an able and learned man, who was the son of an apothecary, and was born in 1714. He was a student of St. John's College, Cambridge. At the early age of twenty-five he was presented to the Chancellorship and a Canonry of Wells. Other preferments rapidly followed, till in 1760 he obtained the Deanery of Bristol, and about a year afterwards was made Bishop of St. Davids, which see he held till his death, May 7, 1766. Dr. Squire was the author of many works on antiquarian, historical, and religious subjects.

A mile or two to the west is the hamlet of *Chapmanslade*, in the parish of *Dilton Marsh*. Its little Independent Chapel, standing by the roadside, reminds us of a remarkable book which appeared in 1856, under the title of *The Autobiography of a Dissenting Minister*. Chapmanslade is the "Willowfield" of the true and interesting story in which the author, who was no other than the now well-known Dr. William Leask, of Maberly Chapel, London, paints with graphic pen the lights and shadows of a Nonconformist 'Country Parson's' life. The volume had a large sale and produced considerable sensation in dissenting circles.

Longleat House forms a conspicuous feature in the fine landscape here. The noble mansion and its history would furnish materials for many a page on which names, many and illustrious, would shine. "Longleate House is the most august building in the Kingdome," was Aubrey's opinion. The estate was purchased, after the Reformation, by Sir John Thynne, who in 1576 commenced the erection of this splendid residence. John of Padua is said to have been the architect, and the works occupied twelve years before the building was complete. Various alterations and additions have since been made by the successive Thynnes who have been its owners. Through many changes it has continued in the same family, John Alexander Thynne, Marquis of Bath, being its present possessor.

A tragic fate befel one of the race in the time of Charles II. Thomas Thynne, nephew of Sir James, was popularly known as "Tom of Ten Thousand," being so called from the supposed amount of his annual income. Some have imagined the appellation was intended to distinguish him above his compeers for the generosity of his disposition and the splendid style of his living. He was a familiar friend of the unfortunate Duke of Monmouth. In 1681 he married Lady Elizabeth Percy, heiress of the 11th Earl of Northumberland, and widow of Lord Ogle. This young creature, who was not more than fifteen years of age, seems to have accepted this second husband unwillingly and under the influence of an unwise mother. One Count Konigsmark, a young Swedish officer, about eight years older than the juvenile widow, who had set his heart upon securing her for himself, plotted a deadly revenge. Some foreign assassins were engaged, and on the night of Sunday, Feb. 12, 1682, Mr. Thynne was barbarously shot as he was riding in his carriage along Pall Mall, from the Countess of Northumberland's to his own London residence. All concerned in the murder were taken ; the chief criminal, Konigsmark, was acquitted; but his three tools were convicted and hanged. A marble monument in Westminster Abbey perpetuates the memory of the unfortunate victim of this tragedy, and bears a *bas relief* representing his murder. On Mr. Thynne's death, Longleat passed to his second cousin, Thomas Thynne, of Kempsford, Gloucestershire, who was immediately created Baron Thynne of Warminster, and first Viscount Weymouth.

It was at Longleat where, for twenty years, he had lived under its hospitable roof, that Bishop Ken finished his mortal course. This devout and amiable prelate, who, by his Evening Hymn, has taught not the Winchester boys only, but thousands of his fellow men, to pray

> " Teach me to live, that I may dread
> The grave as little as my bed!
> To die, that this vile body may
> Rise glorious at the awful day !"

and who so desired to be impressed with a sense of his own mortality that he constantly carried his shroud in his portmanteau, died 19th March, 1711, aged 72. Dr. Merewether, of Devizes, thus records the event in his diary: "March 16th I went to Longleate to visit Bishop Ken,—met Dr. Benson :—18th I waited on him again : *Ibid.* 19th All glory be to God. Between 5 and 6 in yᵉ morning, Thomas, late Bishop of Bath and Wells, died at Longleate." He was buried, according to his own wish, in the nearest parish church of his own diocese, which was that of Frome.

December 10th to 13th, 1881, will have to be added to the red letter days of Longleat archives. On the first of these dates the Prince and Princess of Wales, accepting an invitation from the Marquis of Bath, came on a visit to Longleat House. The royal visitors, who were accompanied by a brilliant retinue, were entertained with magnificent hospitality ; and on their departure expressed their hearty appreciation of their noble host's arrangements for their comfort and pleasure.

In the large and massive old church of *Heytesbury* is a marble tablet to the memory of

WILLIAM CUNNINGTON,

whom the inscription describes as " Fellow of the Society of Antiquaries ; a native of Northamptonshire ; and many years resident in the town of Heytesbury." " By his decease," it is added, " the literary world has lost a persevering antiquary and skilful geologist; the community of Heytesbury a good neighbour and active fellow citizen ; the poor a humane advocate and charitable protector; his own lamenting family an affectionate husband and indulgent parent." This high praise is from the pen of Sir Richard C. Hoare, the great historian of the county, who was on intimate terms of friendship with Mr. Cunnington, and well fitted to bear witness to his acquirements and excellences. It was to Mr. Cunnington that Sir Richard dedicated his work *The History of Ancient Wilts;* a graceful act alike honourable to the baronet and to the man of business. It should be added that Mr. Cunnington, who for some time greatly assisted Mr. Britton in his county researches, also rendered valuable help to Sir Richard Hoare. He died on the last day of 1810, aged 56.

One of the purest and most honourable of the many pure and honourable men belonging to the republican party, in the great struggle with Charles I., was

EDMUND LUDLOW,

a native of *Hill Deverill,* where he was born about 1620. His father was Sir Henry Ludlow, afterwards representative for Wiltshire in the Long Parliament. Edmund became a student at Trinity College, Oxford, and afterwards went to the Temple and studied for the law. On the breaking out of the civil war, he joined Lord Essex's guards, and bore a brave part in the battle of Edge-hill. He was also engaged in the siege of Wardour Castle, of which he was afterwards made Governor; and he subsequently fought at the second battle of Newbury. He was appointed Sheriff of his native county, and on the death of his father succeeded him as its representative in Parliament. Animated by sternly republican principles and aiming at the establishment of a pure Commonwealth, this English Cato opposed some of Cromwell's designs with dignified candour and firmness. To remove him out of the way and lessen his influence he was appointed Commander of the troops in Ireland. When Charles was brought to trial Ludlow formed one of the tribunal by which he was condemned. On Cromwell's assuming the Protectorate, this fearless republican did not fail to express his disapproval of the act, and he was consequently placed under arrest, but at length allowed to retire into private life. After the death of Oliver, he again took his seat in Parliament, but at the restoration of monarchy left England for the continent. He returned after the Revolution had placed William III. on the throne, but Sir Edward Seymour and others taking measures for his apprehension he again left his native land, and died in exile at Vevey, 1693, at the age of 73. A Latin inscription on his house at Vevey is now at Heywood House, near Westbury. It is one worthy of the man : "Omne solum forti patria, quia patris." 1686. It is freely translated by Macaulay " To whom God is a father, every land is a fatherland." His Memoirs, written by himself, in a manly and unaffected style, were published in three volumes a few years after his death. Like those of his great fellow countyman and political opponent, Earl Clarendon, although written from widely opposite standpoints, they furnish much interesting and valuable information as to the events of that most remarkable period of our national history.

JOHN WHITE.

a vicar of *Monkton Deverill*, was ejected by Cromwell's Commissioners. Although thus sequestered, he remained in the neighbourhood, and for several years practised as a medical man. He also published some volumes of poems, which met with much favour at the time of their appearance. He died at Chirton, 1671.

SIR EDWARD SEYMOUR,

the opponent, not to say persecutor, of Ludlow, was by property and residence connected with *Maiden Bradley*, a village about three miles from that which gave the republican birth. Here, too, in the parish church Sir Edward found a resting place, after a somewhat active life, through the eventful periods of the Restoration and the Revolution. His monument, an elaborate work of art in marble, bears a long inscription recording his death in 1707, at the age of 74, and highly eulogising his character. A writer who had but little sympathy with his principles and conduct as a politician, yet honourably testifies that " he was never known to sacrifice his principles for the sake of court-favour, place, or pension." It is satisfactory to find that in all parties there are men who have *not* a price.

We come upon the little town of *Mere* in an angle of the county bordering on Somerset and Dorset. It possesses no remarkable features. " The church," said a writer some seventy years ago, " is the only building here worthy of notice, and this is a spacious edifice with a handsome square tower attached to its west end." Any topographer visiting Mere would, doubtless, refer to another religious building—the Congregational

Chapel—and tell how this beautiful Gothic structure had been erected by the munificence of a townsman, Charles Jupe, Esq.

Here was the birthplace of

FRANCIS, LORD COTTINGTON,

a celebrated statesman in the courts of the first Stuarts. He was born about 1574. Much of his early life was passed in Spain, where he not only acquired a large knowledge of the people and the language, but many of their manners also, particularly their grave and dignified deportment. On his return to England in the reign of James I. he was made Clerk of the Council, but was shortly afterwards sent to Spain on State business, and remained there four years. For this service he was knighted. He became secretary to Prince Charles, but incurred the displeasure of Buckingham, who, as long as he could, prevented his further advancement. On the death of this worthless favourite, about four years after Charles I. had come to the throne, Cottington's prospects brightened, and he was nominated Chancellor and Under Treasurer of the Exchequer. He was sent as ambassador to negotiate a peace with Spain, and being successful in his mission, was created Baron of Hanworth. Further advancement awaited him, and he was made Lord Treasurer and Master of the Court of Wards. He held these high offices till the beginning of the Civil War, when he lost all by his adherence to Royalty. After the King's execution he accompanied Sir Edward Hyde on an embassy to Spain, where he died at Valladolid about 1651. Some writers do not hesitate to assert that all his formal solemnity of deportment was but a cloak for great dissimulation in his political character and career.

FRANCIS POTTER,

a man of a very different order to Cottington, was born at the Vicarage, in the same town, in 1594. Educated for the Church, he succeeded his father in the Rectory of Kilmington. The strong bent of an inquisitive and mechanical genius led him to adopt " a single, monkish" kind of life. Hydraulic machinery especially engaged his attention, and several important discoveries made by him were communicated to the Royal Society, of which he was a member. Other inventions are attributed to him. His curious mind likewise found exercise in a work entitled *An Interpretation of the Apocalyptic Number 666.* Joseph Mede, the noted writer on these mysterious subjects, extravagantly lauded Potter's production as "the happiest book that ever came into the world, and such as cannot be read without admiration." It also "pleased" Pepys "mightily," as being, "whether right or wrong, mighty ingenious." Later critics, however, rank it with the great majority of such works, and consider that it reflects no credit on either his common sense or his ingenuity as a commentator. He found recreation at the easel, and attained to some eminence as a painter. Aubrey, who was his intimate friend, gives many curious anecdotes of him. He became blind, and died 1678, at the age of 82.

The parish of *Stourton* is partly in this county and partly in Somersetshire. Stourhead, a large estate comprised in its bounds, lies wholly in Wilts. It was for many years the property and residence of the Stourtons, of whom there was a long succession of Lords. Charles, the seventh of the line, has obtained infamous notoriety by the murder of one Hartgill and his son, of the neighbouring Somersetshire parish of Kilmington. This foul deed was accomplished by the aid of four of his servants, all of whom, as well as himself, were executed for the crime. Lord Stourton was hanged with a silken halter in Salisbury Market-place, on March 6th, 1556.

The twelfth Lord Stourton sold the estate to Sir Thomas Meres, from whom it was purchased by Henry Hoare, Esq., of London, in 1720. The son of this gentleman bearing the same name was created a baronet. He married a Miss Colt, and was the father of a son who has become known as

SIR RICHARD COLT HOARE,

the topographer and historian of Wiltshire. Sir Richard was born December 9th, 1758, and spent some part of his youthful life in the great banking establishment, Hoare and Co's, Fleet-street, with which the family name has been so long connected. Here he acquired habits of business and industry, which were useful in after life. At the age of twenty-five he married the eldest daughter of Lord Lyttelton, but in about two years was deprived of his young wife by death. Shortly after this event, which occurred in 1785, he went to travel on the Continent, but returned to England and succeeded to the baronetcy in 1787. He again travelled till 1791, making such use of his pen and pencil that on his return he published, at the wish of his friends, *A Classical Tour Through Italy and Sicily*. As writer and as artist he engaged in other works, especially rendering assistance to Archdeacon Coxe, of Bemerton, in his work, *A Tour Through Monmouthshire*, which was embellished with plates from drawings by his pencil. At length he commenced the great undertaking with which his name is now associated, the *History of Wiltshire*. In prosecuting his researches Sir Richard spared neither labour nor expense. As the work proceeded it became his "study, pastime, rest, and food." Valuable coadjutors were found, and the result was the production of elaborate volumes, rich in Wiltshire historical lore. Of *Modern Wiltshire*, consisting of six volumes, a small impression was printed, and perfect sets are comparatively few in number: *Ancient Wiltshire* is not so voluminous. For more than thirty years the best energies of Sir Richard's active and generous mind were devoted to this work.

As life advanced his mind and pen continued to be well employed, and in his last years he wrote a pleasing autobiography. He died in his eightieth year, May 19th, 1838, and lies buried in the mausoleum of the Hoare family in the secluded churchyard of Stourton. In the upper park an obelisk ninety feet in height has been erected to his memory.

Wiltshire men may well feel a pardonable pride as they gaze on that magnificent pile—St. Paul's Cathedral: its great architect was a Wiltshire man.

SIR CHRISTOPHER WREN

was the son of Dr. Christopher Wren, rector of *East Knoyle*, and was born, in a house still standing, on October 20th, 1632. His father as a royalist incurred the displeasure of the Parliament and was proceeded against as a 'Delinquent.' He was also charged with superstitious practices in his church—having pictures of the four evangelists and others therein. He appears to have been leniently dealt with, the Committee of Lords and Commons for sequestration suggesting to the Wilts Committee to treat him with tenderness as being a "person far from meriting the doom of sequestration."

The education of young Christopher was commenced at a private school, but he afterwards entered Wadham College, Oxford. He gave early proof of great mathematical genius, and before he was sixteen years old was able to solve the most difficult problems in geometry. At the age of twenty-five he was chosen professor of astronomy in Gresham College. Charles II. appointed him a Surveyor of the Board of Works, and he was shortly afterwards elected a Fellow of the Royal Society. On the appearance of the plague in London in 1665, he went to France, where he diligently spent his time in the study of architecture. On his return the following year he found two-thirds of London in ruins, having been destroyed by the great fire. He proposed a plan for so rebuilding the city that the new cathedral should occupy a centre from which the great thoroughfares should run in direct lines. This design was abandoned owing to disputes among the owners of private property. Wren, however, undertook the erection of the cathedral, which noble work was finished in 1710; and St. Paul's now stands the most magnificent Protestant church in the world.

The Monument was also his work, as well as many other public buildings, including a great number of churches, Greenwich Hospital, and Chelsea Hospital, the last of which he executed without fee or reward, in order to promote the benevolent purposes for which it was built.

The genius and pursuits of Sir Christopher were unfavourable to an active political life, and although twice returned to Parliament, once for Plympton, in Devon, and again for Weymouth and Melcombe Regis unitedly, he never took any lively or distinguished part in state affairs. The latter part of his life was passed in great tranquillity, and he reached the advanced age of ninety-one, dying February 25th, 1723. The great creation of his architectural genius became his last resting place, his body being buried with due honours under the choir of the cathedral. By a happy inspiration a Latin epitaph on a pillar near his tomb makes his own great work the monument of his fame and memory :

Lector, si Monumentum quæris, Circumspice.

Reader, if thou seekest his monument, look around.

Although the fame of Sir Christopher rests chiefly on his architectural productions, his character as a man of general science was very high, and his discoveries in astronomy and other branches of natural philosophy were such as rank him among the great benefactors of mankind.

Sir Christopher is credited with an invention which from a curious cause he seems never to have made public. "John Aubrey" says a recent writer, "tells us that Sir Christopher Wren produced 'a way to weave 7 paire or 9 paire of stockings at once (it must be an odd number).' The great architect demanded of the silk stocking-weavers £400 for his invention, but they would not buy it because they were poor, 'and besides they sayde it would spoyle their trade.' 'Perhaps,' continues Aubrey, 'they did not consider the proverb that light gains with quick returns, make heavy purses.' Sir Christopher was so noble, seeing that they would not adventure so much money, 'he breakes the modell of the engine all to pieces before their faces,' which was, perhaps, as sensible and well-advised a course as he could well take."

The story of Fonthill Abbey and its eccentric proprietor,

WILLIAM BECKFORD,

has been often told. The father of this gentleman was a distinguished citizen of London, and was born 1705. He was engaged in merchandise, but took an active part in the affairs of the city, and was twice elected Lord Mayor. He became possessed of the manor of *Fonthill Gifford* by descent from the Mervins, and at great cost built in 1755 a splendid mansion, which he surrounded with fine grounds and gardens. He died in 1770, leaving his vast property to his still more remarkable son, then a boy ten years of age. William, who received an education becoming his station, gave early signs of genius. The brilliant Eastern romance of *Vathek* was written by him in French at the age of twenty-two. "It took me," he said, "three days and two nights of hard labour. I never took off my clothes the whole time." Fonthill scenes and characters ideally exaggerated were largely wrought into the story. In 1783 he married Lady Margaret Gordon, daughter of the Earl of Aboyne. He was elected representative for Hindon in 1790. About the beginning of the century he commenced making great changes at Fonthill, erecting sumptuous buildings, including a tower 260 feet high. In 1822 he disposed of the estate, and retired to Lansdowne near Bath, where he lived in eccentric splendour. He died in 1844.

Wardour Castle, the seat of Lord Arundell of Wardour, is in the parish of *Tisbury*. It was built about a century ago. The ruins of the old castle standing at a short distance form a prominent feature in the scenery. They also remind us of the time of civil strife, and of

LADY BLANCH ARUNDELL,

wife of the second Lord Arundell. This nobleman while attending Charles I. at Oxford left the castle in the custody of Lady Blanch. It was soon afterwards besieged by Sir Edward Hungerford, with a Parliamentarian force 1300 strong. With a garrison of only twenty-five men, the heroic lady withstood the besiegers for five days, and then surrendered only upon most honourable terms. The castle was immediately garrisoned by the Parliamentarians, under command of Edmund Ludlow. A siege by the Royalists, led by Lord Arundell, followed, and after a brave and determined resistance of several weeks, it capitulated. It was then greatly injured; and Lord Arundell enraged at its having been in the possession of the Parliamentarians, and probably fearing its again falling into their hands, entirely dismantled it. It is probable that the old castle was the birth-place of

SIR NICHOLAS HYDE,

who was Chief Justice of the King's Bench and Lord Treasurer of England in the reign of Charles I. He was uncle to Earl Clarendon, and assisted him in his legal studies. He occupied his high stations only a few years, dying in 1631.

Chicksgrove, one of the hamlets of the large parish of Tisbury, was the birthplace of

SIR JOHN DAVIES,

an eminent lawyer, poet, and political writer, who was born about 1570. He was the son of a solicitor. When fifteen years of age, he was admitted a commoner of Queen's College, Oxford. He afterwards entered the Middle Temple, London, where, conducting himself with some irregularity, he was expelled in 1597. Retiring to Oxford, and apparently deeply regretting his past follies, he wrote a remarkable poem, *Nosce Teipsum*, Know Thyself. This work, which was dedicated to Queen Elizabeth, may be numbered among the literary marvels of the age, and has obtained for him the title of a philosophical poet. Profound questions, relating to human knowledge and the soul, are discussed with great ingenuity of reasoning, and yet with singular clearness and beauty. Reference to his own indiscretions and consequent troubles is made in some quatrains, of which the following is the first :—

> "If aught can teach us aught, Affliction's looks
>   (Making us pry into ourselves so near),
> Teach us to know ourselves, beyond all books,
>   Or all the learned schools that ever were."

He sat in the parliament that assembled in 1601, and took a liberal interest in the welfare of the people. In the same year, his own apology and the influence of powerful friends secured his restoration to his old rank in the Temple. He was now a rapidly rising man, both in his profession and in public life. On the death of Elizabeth, in 1603, he accompanied Lord Hunsdon when that nobleman went to Scotland to congratulate James I. upon his accession to the British throne. The king ascertaining that he was the author of *Nosce Teipsum*, gave him not only a flattering welcome, but also promises of his patronage and support. He was soon appointed Attorney-General for Ireland, and in 1606 received the honour of knighthood. Other honours followed, and in December, 1626, he was raised to the dignity of Lord Chief Justice of the King's Bench, but died of apoplexy on the 7th of the same month.

Of Lady Davies, who from all accounts appears to have been an insane person, Aubrey says : " Sir John's Lady was a Prophetess, or rather Witch, who was kept Prisoner in the Tower for her seditious predictions. Mathew Davys has told me severall strange stories of his aunt ; one that her husband being then in Ireland, or far remote, she told the very hour of his death."

To many readers in various parts of the world, Tisbury has become known as the birthplace of the Rev.

WILLIAM JAY,

for many years one of the most widely known and highly esteemed nonconformist preachers in the kingdom.   He was born May 8th, 1769.   His parents were of good character, but in humble circumstances, his father being a stone cutter and mason.   His home was a thatched cottage, his father's own property, and was situated, he tells us—"about an equal distance from Wardour Castle, Pithouse, and Fonthill."   " The village in which it stood," he adds with a loving appreciation of its pleasant scenes, " was wide and varied, and abounded with lovely and picturesque aspects—

'And the sweet interchange of hill and vale and wood and lawn.' "

Having obtained such education as the village school afforded he began to follow the occupation of his father, with whom he worked at the erection of Fonthill Abbey.   Attracting the notice of Cornelius Winter, who was at that time minister of the Independent Chapel at Marlborough, and occasionally preached at Tisbury, he became a student in the house of that benevolent man, of whom he afterwards said—

" Loved as his son, in him I early found
A father, such as I will ne'er forget."

When little more than sixteen he preached his first sermon at Ablington, a village near Stonehenge, and from this time " the Boy Preacher," as he was called, was in such request that before he was twenty-one he had delivered nearly a thousand sermons.   Soon after he had commenced preaching some of his friends who were contributing to his educational expenses were desirous for him to go to the University and enter the Church. Instead of this he became pastor of the little chapel at Christian Malford at a salary of £35 a year. He was, however, boarded gratuitously by a generous tradesman, and was " therefore as to accommodation and provision perfectly satisfied, and free from all worldly care." The following year, at the earnest request of Lady Maxwell, he became preacher at Hope Chapel, Clifton. In 1791 he removed to Bath, being chosen minister of Argyle Chapel, at the opening of which he had preached two years before. Here he attracted great attention, and gained a large number of admirers and friends. Lady Huntingdon, Hannah More, Mr. John Thornton, Mr. Wilberforce, Mr. Beckford, and many others of high rank and refined taste, held him in great esteem as a man and a preacher. His discourses were unique. While interesting the educated they were easily understood by the poor and illiterate. This resulted in great measure from the freshness of his thoughts, the clearness of his language, and the happy and homely illustrations he so freely used, all combined with a pleasing appearance and manner. Struck with the flowing originality of his mind, Beckford remarked, " He is not a reservoir, he is a fountain." Dr. Redford and Mr. James, themselves eminent preachers, describe " his talent for illus- trative allusion" as extraordinary. " His sermons," they say, " were not only by his beautiful fancy illuminated like the ancient missals, but illustrated like modern books by descriptive scenes. They contained all the glowing colouring of the one, with the more correct and graceful forms of the other. Here his naturalness constantly appeared, and in close resemblance to that of our Lord, who drew his similes and metaphors from the works of nature and the relationships of humanity."

A Wiltshire gentleman related the following incident as affording a specimen of the simplicity of his style and the felicity of his illustrations. Preaching on one occasion at Devizes, and exhorting his hearers to "patient continuance in well doing," he said "As I came through your streets this morning I saw some children playing, and as they played they marched and sang—

> ' One foot up and one foot down,
> That's the way to London town;' "

and then added with impressive earnestness, "Ah! I thought to myself, and that is how it must be with the Christian pilgrim—

> ' One foot up and one foot down,
> For *that's* the way to Zion town!' "

The Jubilee of Mr. Jay's pastorate was celebrated in 1841, and was a remarkable and interesting occasion. Churchmen joined with dissenters in showing him esteem and doing him honour. In 1845 he experienced a great trial in the death of his wife after a happy union of fifty-four years' duration. By a judicious second marriage the comfort of his last years was greatly promoted. There are few thoughtful people who would willingly re-tread life's path, but Mr. Jay, in his old age, reviewed life with so much satisfaction that he expressed his willingness to live it over again! Acknowledging "Goodness and mercy have followed me all the days of my life," and enumerating many of its favourable conditions, he concludes—

> "Call not earth a barren spot,
> Pass it not unheeded by;
> 'Tis to man a lovely spot,
> Though a lovelier waits on high."

His course was, doubtless, exceptionally smooth and prosperous.

Mr. Jay was an extensive author; and his works excellent as well as numerous obtained a wide circle of readers of nearly all classes and creeds. His life of Cornelius Winter is a model piece of biography. For some years before his death he resided at Bradford-on-Avon, where he closed his long and useful life, Dec. 27, 1853, at the age of 85. His memoirs, consisting chiefly of an autobiography, were edited by his friends the Rev. John Angell James, of Birmingham, and the Rev. Dr. Redford, of Worcester.

The village of *Semley*, lying in a beautiful valley, was the birthplace of

WILLIAM THORN,

who rose to celebrity as a linguist and divine. In 1598 he was appointed Professor of Hebrew in the University of Oxford. For his knowledge of this language he was particularly distinguished. A few years afterwards he was preferred to the deanery of Chichester, where he continued till his death in 1629, and where he was buried in the Cathedral.

Let it be recorded to the honour of the Rev.

JOHN GANE,

a rector of *Berwick St. John*, that "by his will dated 1735, he left a tenement and garden, on condition that the great bell of the parish church should be rung for a quarter of an hour at eight o'clock every night from the 10th of September to the 10th of March, for ever, for the purpose of enabling travellers on the Wiltshire downs to find their way by the sound on dark and foggy nights."

PART III.

MID WILTS.—*SOUTH.*

" Pitch thy behaviour low, thy projects high :
    So shalt thou humble and magnanimous be ;
Sink not in spirit : who aimeth at the sky
    Shoots higher much than he that means a tree.
    A grain of glorie mixt with humblenesse
    Cures both a fever and lethargicknesse.

" Let thy mind still be bent, still plotting where,
    And when, and how the businesse may be done.
Slacknesse breeds worms ; but the sure traveller,
    Though he alight sometimes, still goeth on.
    Active and stirring spirits live alone :
    Write on the others, Here lies such a one."

GEORGE HERBERT.

" Happy are those,
That knowing in their birth, they are subject to
Uncertain changes, are still prepared and arm'd
For either fortune : a rare principle,
And with much labour learn'd in wisdom's school."

PHILIP MASSINGER.

E are now in the lower part of the county, where the chases of Cranborne and Vernditch and the southern downs running from east to west, watered by sparkling streams, form peculiarly charming scenery. "I like it," said Charles Kingsley, writing in the midst of it to his wife, " better than Devon or Welsh moorland—it is more simple, and yet not so severe—more tender in its soft greys and greens, yet quite as sublime in the vast unbroken curves and sweeps of the open downs. I cannot express myself. I should like to preach a sermon on chalk downs, and another on chalk streams. They are so *purely* beautiful."

F 2

Dr. Stanford, in a work to which we shall presently refer more fully, reminds us that Sir Walter Raleigh sometimes resided in the neighbourhood of *Damerham*, in the most southerly point of the county, where " One day, after his morning walk amidst fern, and white-thorn, and starting deer, along the ancient chase, and by the brimming river, he is said to have written the following verses to describe the scene of his rambles :—

> ' Abused mortals ! did you know
> Where joy, heart's-ease, and comforts grow,
>   You'd scorn proud towers,
>   And seek them in these bowers ;
> Where winds sometimes our words perhaps may shake,
> But blustering care could never tempests make,
>   Nor murmurs e'er come nigh us,
>   Saving of fountains that glide by us.
>
> Blest silent groves ! O may ye be
> For ever mirth's best nursery !
>   May pure contents
>   For ever pitch their tents
> Upon these downs, these meads, these rocks, these mountains,
> And peace still slumber by these purling fountains,
>   Which we may every year
>   Find when we come a-fishing here.'

Amidst these scenes of quietude and beauty

WILLIAM RHODES,

who is the subject of the volume quoted from, was born in the year 1792. He was the son of a village carpenter, and his childhood was one of poverty and sorrows resulting from the intemperance of his father. At seven years of age he went to work—toiling as a child should never toil—at various rural employments, till at twelve he began to learn his father's business. Six years rough labour much shattered his health, and grave cares gave an abiding melancholy tinge to his habits of thought. About this time, while working at Ringwood, his mind underwent a great religious change. Some months after this he was baptised at Salisbury by the Rev. J. Saffery. He began to preach, and was soon sent as a student to the Baptist College at Bristol. From Bristol he went to Edinburgh University, where he formed an intimate acquaintance with Dr. Brown, then Professor of Moral Philosophy.

He left Edinburgh with a weak body and a still weaker voice, and became pastor of a little Baptist church at the village of Sherfield, in Hampshire. This step was unsatisfactory. He found himself among ultra-Calvinists, who would neither think nor work, their souls having "retired to rest and drawn the curtains." At the end of six months he resigned his charge and retired to his native village. In 1823 he suffered from fever, and for six months his life hung in a balance. He was slowly restored to strength, "and then, partly working at his original trade, and partly by means of a small income which he received from a friend, in acknowledgment of inestimable spiritual services, he contrived not only to live free from the worst effects of poverty himself, but to be a generous benefactor to others. In the course of the next few years he built a cottage for his sisters; he also received into his house some afflicted relatives, and was their watchful attendant and sole supporter till they died." In addition to this he gathered together a few farm servants, to whom he became a true pastor. This humble effort so prospered that in 1829 a chapel was erected. The people supplied many of the materials and much of the labour; the pastor himself making the whole of its humble furniture, and also paying £50, the total pecuniary cost, out of his own narrow means. "Here he ministered to the end of his days, not only without the slightest worldly remuneration, but meeting from his own resources every incidental expense."

Mr. Rhodes had reached his fortieth year when he married Miss Hester Knight, a lady of Devizes. This happy union greatly contributed to his comfort and usefulness. As life advanced his afflictions increased, and at length paralysis rendered even writing a difficult operation. His rare powers of mind were, however, still exercised in thought and conversation. What these powers were may be partly learned from the specimens of his writings which his biography contains. The singular beauty of his character increased with age and infirmities, and shone most brightly as he neared the end. Among the last words his pencil ever traced were these :—"Let us labour and aspire to make the last stage of our pilgrimage more worthy of our great prospects in the world to come." The 7th of May, 1856, a few days after these words were written, his sufferings and his life peacefully ended. The Rev. Richard Allnutt, vicar of Damerham, "esteeming it a privilege if he could say anything to enhance and perpetuate the respect entertained for this excellent servant of God by every parishioner," preached a sermon on the occasion of his funeral. The text selected was "Well done, good and faithful servant," &c., and the discourse was afterwards published.

The volume to which we have already referred and from which these particulars have been gathered, is entitled *Power in Weakness. Memorials of the Rev. William Rhodes, of Damerham. By Charles Stanford.* It was written during the residence of Dr. Stanford as Baptist minister at Devizes, and is an admirable piece of biography.

Broadchalk was the birthplace of

JOHN BEKINSAU,

who took an active part in the Reformation during the times of Henry VIII. and Edward VI. On the accession of Mary he professedly changed his religion to suit changed circumstances, so that at the close of her short reign and the return of Protestant supremacy, he retired into private life under the disgrace which his conduct had incurred. He was reputed one of the most learned men of his time, and especially eminent for his Greek scholarship. He was an intimate friend of Leland. His death occurred at Sherborne, in Hampshire, in 1559.

ROBERT BATEMAN WRAY

was born at Broadchalk in 1715. His father, a descendant of Sir Christopher Wray, Lord Chief Justice of England, was vicar of the parish. Robert became a gem engraver; and by his taste and skill in this art acquired much celebrity. His head of the dying Cleopatra, which he deemed his most perfect work, was sold for a trifling sum to the Duke of Northumberland. He died at Salisbury in 1779, and was buried in the porch of St. Edmund's Church.

Four miles west of Broadchalk is the little village of *Ansty*, almost encompassed by downs, and possessing a church which, before its restoration, was viewed by archæologists with great interest as without exception the oldest in the whole diocese. Here, towards the end of the sixteenth century, was born

DR. RICHARD ZOUCH,

son of an ancient and noble family whose name was connected with many places in the county. He was a Winchester scholar, and afterwards a student of New College, Oxford. He practised in Doctors' Commons, attaining such distinction that in 1619 he was nominated Regius Professor of Civil Law. After entering parliament he became Chancellor of the Diocese of Oxford, and subsequently Judge of the High Court of Admiralty. He retained all his appointments, except the last, during the Commonwealth, and died in March, 1660. His writings comprise works on feudal-canon, ecclesiastical, and herald laws.

HENRY PENRUDDOCKE WYNDHAM,

born at *Compton Chamberlain* in 1736, received his education at Eton, and Wadham College, Oxford. He visited many parts of the continent, and afterwards travelled much in England and Wales, publishing *Two Tours made in Monmouthshire and Wales in* 1774 *and* 1777, and also a *Description of the Isle of Wight.* He was among the most intelligent and assiduous topographers and local historians of that day; and was particularly zealous in elucidating the history and antiquities of his native county. With this view he printed in 1788 the *Account of Wiltshire from Domesday,* with a translation. In his preface he suggested a plan for a County History on an extensive scale. This was to some extent accomplished by the labours of Sir R. C. Hoare, who was much assisted in his work by Mr. Wyndham's researches.

Mr. Wyndham was Mayor of Salisbury in 1771, and in 1772 Sheriff of Wilts. He was chosen M.P. for the County in 1796 and retained his seat till the infirmities of age obliged him to resign it in 1812. He was a great favourite of George III., and an anecdote is told of his appearing at Court on one occasion in a coat made of dark striped coloured cloth. The King thinking it was a French cloth which was then much worn, exclaimed "What Wyndham in a French coat!" "No; please your Majesty it is not French." "What then?" "It is a cloth made at Salisbury." "Then send me some of it." This was done and the material being thus made fashionable its manfacture became a source of much occupation and profit to the Salisbury people. Mr. Wyndham died May 3, 1819.

The excellent freestone quarries in the parish of *Chilmark* are said to have supplied the greater part of the stone used in the building of Salisbury Cathedral, and many of the churches in the southern part of the county. The little village is noted as having given birth and name to a celebrated mathematician and philosophical writer of the thirteenth century,

JOHN DE CHILMARKE.

He studied at Merton College, Oxford. Great talents joined with patient industry enabled him to attain such proficiency in geometrical science, that "he was accounted," says an old writer, "the Archimedes of that age." He wrote several works.

JAMES LEY, EARL OF MARLBOROUGH,

was the sixth son of a gentleman of *Teffont Ewyas*, where he was born about 1552. According to Aubrey, he was made vicar of Teffont when about seventeen years of age, the living, which was worth £60 a year, serving to support him at Brasennose College, Oxford. His clerical duties were performed by proxy. "The Butler, or somebody, read the Prayers." On leaving Oxford he removed to Lincoln's Inn. Being called to the bar he rapidly rose to various important offices, and was knighted by James I. He became Chief Justice of the King's Bench, and four years afterwards Lord High Treasurer. He was also raised to the peerage as Lord Ley, of Ley, Devonshire, and on the accession of Charles I. was advanced to the dignity of the Earl of Marlborough. Wealth came with honours, as by the demise of his five eldest brothers he came into possession of the whole paternal estate. He purchased large property at Westbury, and like a good proprietor, was concerned for the moral condition of the town.

Writing to John Hall, Esq., Magistrate and M.P. for Westbury, in 1607, he says " Our town of Westbury hath need of you to see to the corruption that useth to grow in such places. I pray you take some care of our drinkers : and since the King hath made some good laws against that vice, I hope that you that be magistrates will not suffer it to encrease more than when there were no laws against it."

The Earl was thrice married, and when he died in 1628, at the age of 76, he left " a young, beautiful, and rich widow." He lies buried under a sumptuous monument in Westbury Church, and is celebrated by Milton as

> " That good Earl, once president
> Of England's Council and her Treasury."

The parish register of *Dinton*, dating from the time of Elizabeth, contains the name of

HENRY LAWES,

as christened here, where he was probably born, New Year's Day, 1595. Those who are acquainted with the history of English music will remember Lawes as a musician of some celebrity in the time of Charles I., the Commonwealth, and after the Restoration. His father was Thomas Lawes, a vicar-choral in Salisbury Cathedral. " The quire of Salisbury Cathedral hath produced as many able musicians," says Aubrey, " if not more than any quire in this nation." Young Lawes was one of these. He early became celebrated as a performer and composer, and was appointed one of Charles the First's private musicians. During the Commonwealth he supported himself by teaching music. Milton, Waller, and other poets admired his genius, and were ambitious to have their compositions set to music by him. His praises are thus sung by Milton, who is said to have written *Comus* at his suggestion :—

> " Harry, whose tuneful and well-measur'd song
> First taught our English music how to span
> Words with just note and accent."

The anthem at the coronation of Charles II. was his composition. He died 1662.

In the same parish register, under date Feb. 22, 1608, appears another name destined to be afterwards written conspicuously in the annals of the eventful century which was then in its infancy. It is that of

EDWARD HYDE, EARL OF CLARENDON,

who had been born at Dinton House, or in its vicinity, on the 18th of the same month. His father, who was a man of great capacity and high principle, after frequently sitting in parliament during the reign of Elizabeth, retired from public life at her death, and devoted himself to the improvement of his estates and the education of his family. In the latter he was assisted by the vicar of the parish, under whose tuition young Edward obtained the elements of learning, till at fourteen he went to Oxford. He was intended for the Church but circumstances led to his studying for the law. Entering the Middle Temple, he pursued his legal studies under the guidance of his uncle, Sir Nicholas Hyde. At the same time he made good progress in classical and general knowledge. While quite young he formed friendships with several of the most eminent men of the time; and was ever careful to avoid the intimate acquaintance of any who were not esteemed for their talents and their virtues.

In 1640 he was returned to parliament for the borough of Wootton Bassett; and soon excited attention and admiration by a speech against the practices of the Marshal's court. While loyal to the King he yet gained the confidence of the Commons. With great purity of intention and in the exercise of high abilities, he endeavoured on the one hand to check the imprudent and unconstitutional encroachments of the Crown, and on the other to restrain and moderate the discontent and demands of the people. On the commencement of war he attached himself to the King's party, and was nominated Chancellor of the Exchequer and member of the Privy Council, at the same time receiving the honour of Knighthood. After the battle of Naseby he accompanied the young Prince Charles to Jersey, where, when the prince had gone to France, he remained two years, during which he commenced his principal work, which he entitled *The History of the Great Rebellion*. He continued abroad, chiefly in the service of Charles, till the Restoration, when returning to England he held the office of Lord Chancellor and was made a peer with the title of Earl of Clarendon. Occupying such a high position he was regarded both at home and abroad as the king's first and most confidental minister.

Bishop Burnet's reference to the Earl at this period throws much light upon his position and character. "The King," he says, "was so given up to pleasure, that he devolved the management of all his affairs on the Earl of Clarendon, who as he had his breeding in the law so he had all along declared himself for the ancient liberties of England, as well as for the rights of the Crown. A domestic accident had happened to him which heightened his zeal for the former. He, when he had begun to grow eminent in his profession, came to see his aged father, a gentleman of Wiltshire, who, one day as they were walking in the field together, told him that men of his profession did often stretch law and prerogative, to the prejudice of the subject to recommend and advance themselves. So he charged him if ever he grew to eminence in his profession that he should never sacrifice the laws and liberties of his country to his own interests or to the will of a Prince. He repeated this twice, and immediately fell into a fit of apoplexy, of which he died in a few hours. This the Earl of Clarendon told the Lady Ranelagh, who put him afterwards in mind of it ; and from her I had it."

In the "merry monarch" he had a fickle and unworthy master; the corruptions of the court caused him much disquiet; and he had many unscrupulous enemies. Occasion was found against him. The king's brother, James Duke of York, while visiting his sister the Princess of Orange, at Breda, fell in love with Anne Hyde, Earl Clarendon's eldest daughter, who was maid of honour to the Princess. A private marriage, of which Clarendon was as ignorant as Charles, took place in November, 1659. This event, which did not become known till after the Restoration, was used by the Earl's enemies to his disadvantage. The king, however, professed no displeasure, but on being satisfied of the validity of the marriage, he acknowledged Anne as Duchess of York and declared his unlessened confidence in her father. Other difficulties and troubles followed, till the King, whose real feelings had probably been concealed, became openly displeased. This displeasure soon grew to hatred as

Clarendon expostulated with the licentious monarch upon his evil courses, and especially upon his shameful treatment of the Queen. Things were brought to a climax by the Earl effecting a marriage between the Duke of Richmond and the beautiful Lady Stuart, as Charles had formed a plan to repudiate his own wife and marry the lady himself. Clarendon was deprived of his offices and an impeachment for high treason was commenced against him. He fled to France in 1667, where in retirement at Montpelier he resumed his literary labours with avidity and enjoyed the society of many distinguised men. His years of exile were ended at Rouen, Dec. 7, 1674. It is some satisfaction to know that the remains of this high principled and patriotic Englishman were afterwards brought to his beloved native land, and laid to rest in Westminster Abbey.

It is worthy of record that from this Wiltshire worthy two of our English Queens descended; the daughters of the Duchess of York both coming to the throne—one as Mary, wife of William III., and the other as Queen Anne.

The town of *Wilton* is pleasantly situated near the confluence of the Wiley and the Nadder. From the former river it derives its name, and then gives name to the shire of which it was in olden days a chief place. It is historically interesting, having been the scene of many remarkable events. It is commonly believed that the first carpets manufactured in England were made here. The maker was Anthony Duffosy, who was brought from France by Lord Pembroke about the middle of last century. The manufacture is still carried on, and employs a large number of hands.

Two ecclesiastics,

JOHN OF WILTON, *Senior*,

a learned Augustine friar, who lived in the time of Edward II., and

JOHN OF WILTON, *Junior*,

a Benedictine Monk, and an elegant writer, who lived in the reign of Edward III., are reckoned among the eminent natives of the town. A more notable man than either of these,

THOMAS OF WILTON,

flourished in the time of the fourth Edward. As a man of great learning and ability he was first appointed Chancellor and afterwards Dean of St. Paul's, in London. Like Wycliffe he was a strong opponent of the friars, and wrote with great vigour against the Mendicant fraternity. His searching examination of their claims resulted in the unfavourable verdict that they "were rogues by the laws of God and man, and fitter for the House of Correction than the State of Perfection," so Fuller tells us.

High and varied kinds of interest cluster round Wilton House, the famous and beautiful seat of the Herbert family. Originally an abbey, it became the property of William Herbert, Earl of Pembroke, after the dissolution. His son Henry, his successor in the peerage, took for a third wife Mary, daughter of Sir Henry Sidney, and sister of Philip Sidney, "the stainless representative of the young manhood of Elizabethan England." In the early spring of 1580, Philip, then about twenty-five, visited his sister the Countess of Pembroke at her Wiltshire home. The visit extended into November. Brother and sister possessed similar tastes, and worked together at a translation of the Psalms of David into verse. Other portions of Sidney's leisure were spent in writing, solely for the entertainment of his sister, his now well-known pastoral romance, *Arcadia*. It is pleasant to picture the handsome and gifted young knight wandering in the groves and gardens of his temporary abode, or strolling among the fair scenes of the surrounding country, weaving into song the fancies and conceits of his fertile brain. Aubrey helps us to do this when he writes:—"In this tract is ye Earle of Pembroke's noble seat at Wilton; but the Arcadia and the Daphne is about Vernditch and Wilton; and these romancy plaines and boscages did no doubt conduce to the hightening of Sir Philip Sydney's phansie. He lived much in these parts, and his most masterly touches of his pastoralls he wrote here upon the spott, where they were conceived. 'Twas about these purlieus that the muses were wont to appeare to Sir Philip Sydney, and where he wrote down their dictates in his table book, though on horseback. I remember some old relations of mine, and other old men hereabout that have seen Sir Philip doe this."

His sister, the Countess, to whom he was so affectionately attached, was a lady of considerable note. To her many virtues were added great accomplishments and gifts of a high order. Spenser honoured her as

> " The gentlest shepheardesse, that lives this day,
> And most resembling, both in shape and spright,
> Her brother deare."

MARY, COUNTESS OF PEMBROKE.

Several of her productions, in manuscript, are in the Library of the British Museum: one is a remarkable poem entitled " *Our Saviour's Passion*," of which some beautiful stanzas have been published. Her epitaph, written by William Browne, is one of much beauty :—

> " Underneath this sable hearse
> Lies the subject of all verse,
> Sidney's sister, Pembroke's mother:
> Death, ere thou hast slain another,
> Learn'd and fair and good as she,
> Time shall throw a dart at thee."

The Pembroke, to whom the poet refers, was her eldest son,

WILLIAM HERBERT,

third Earl, who was born at Wilton, April 8, 1580, a few days after Sir Philip had arrived on his visit. He was educated at Oxford, and became Chancellor of that University in 1618. Possessed of great learning himself he was also the patron of it in others. Lord Clarendon, whose own estimate of him was high, describes him as "the most universally beloved and esteemed of any man of that age." He indulged his love of literature by writing some poetical pieces which he published jointly with others written by his friend, Sir Benj. Rudyard. A few of his songs were set to music by his neighbour, Henry Lawes. He died in 1630.

The name of the late Right Honourable

SIDNEY HERBERT, FIRST BARON OF LEA,

will long brightly shine in the annals of Wiltshire Worthies. This truly noble man was the son of the eleventh Earl of Pembroke, and was born in 1810. Having passed through Harrow, he graduated at Oxford in 1831, and the following year was returned as Conservative member for South Wilts. During the Anti-Corn Law agitation his political views underwent considerable change, and he took his place among the earliest supporters of Sir Robert Peel when that statesman adopted a broader commercial policy. His services were secured by the administrations of Sir Robert Peel, Lord Aberdeen and Lord Palmerston ; and he displayed great ability in the offices he filled. It was while holding that of Secretary of War during the Crimean campaign, that he sought the aid of Florence Nightingale on behalf of the suffering soldiers in hospital ; and it is an interesting fact that his letter asking her help was crossed by one from that lady voluntarily offering her invaluable services.

Lord Herbert's christian benevolence was ever active in efforts for the promotion of education and the support and spread of religious institutions. The Church of England had no friend more enlightened or munificent. On his estates in Ireland he built, endowed or repaired numerous schools and churches. The magnificent Byzantine Church at Wilton was erected by him at a cost of £30,000 ; while schools and churches in various parts of Wiltshire were aided in their erection, endowment, or restoration by his liberal benefactions. In all these works of benevolence, especially in those on behalf of the sick and wounded Crimean soldiers, he found a true helpmeet in Lady Herbert, daughter of General A'Court, whom he married in 1846.

On the 15th January 1861 he was created Baron Herbert of Lea in the County of Wilts ; but his health weakened by his official labours was even then suffering, and his death took place on August 2nd of the same year.

A beautiful passage, by a recent writer, suggestive of points of re- semblance between Sir Philip Sidney and Lord Herbert, shall close this brief sketch. "An old chronicler thus sums up his estimate of Sir Philip Sidney. 'Certain it is, that he was a noble and matchless gentleman, of whom it may be justly written, without hyperbole or fiction, that he seemed born to do that only which he went about. To speak more of him were to speak less.' These words well stamp the later kinsman of that old 'crown and flower' of English manhood ; and the last lines of the elder Sidney's epitaph would fit with curious felicity the tablet of Sidney Lord Herbert of Lea—

"Heaven hath his soul, the arts his fame,
All soldiers his grief, the world his good name.'"

All this locality is fragrant with the name of

GEORGE HERBERT,

and as we move towards the little hamlet of *Bemerton*, thoughts of the sweet and serious poet crowd upon us. " I spent a delightful day yesterday ;" wrote Charles Kingsley in the spring of 1844. " Conceive my pleasure at finding myself at Bemerton—George Herbert's parish, and seeing his house and church, and fishing in the very meadows where he, and Dr. Donne, and Izaak Walton, may have fished before me." Although not a native of the county, Herbert's name and memory are indissolubly associated with Wiltshire. It was at Dauntsey that he sought change of climate, when signs of consumption began to show in his enfeebled frame. He was affectionately welcomed and entertained at the house of Lord Danby. The result of his visit has been thus pleasantly told : " In this choice air, as Aubrey calls it, by avoiding severe study, and partaking of cheerful exercise and society, his health returned. A new scene was now to open before him. There lived at Bainton, in the same county, a kinsman of Lord Danby, Mr. Charles Danvers. He had nine daughters, of whom Jane was his favourite. To her he had often spoken of Herbert, and promised a double blessing upon the union he hoped to see. It happened that Mr. Danvers died before Herbert's visit to Dauntsey, but as we learn from Walton, Jane, " became so much a Platonick as to fall in love with Mr. Herbert unseen." The smallest spark would light such a train. The only obstacle was the want of acquaintance.

G

This was easily removed. Some mutual friends procured a meeting, and within three days of the first interview, Jane Danvers changed her name into Herbert."

Though thus " marrying in haste," he had no cause for "repenting at leisure." It was a blessed wedded life. A few months after his marriage the rectory of Bemerton becoming vacant, his kinsman, the Earl Pembroke, of Wilton, asked it for him of King James, its patron. "Most willingly to Mr. Herbert, if it be worthy of his acceptance," was the monarch's immediate reply. Herbert was staying at Bainton, but on receiving the news went at once to Wilton. He had known nothing of the Earl's application, and being taken by surprise he hesitated whether to accept the living or not; shrinking with tender conscience from the responsibilities which a cure of souls involves. The reasoning of Laud, then Bishop of London, who was on a visit at Wilton, convinced him that he ought not to refuse. The next day, habited in a suit of canonical garments which had been hastily made for him, he received institution from Bishop Davenant, and on the same day, April 26, 1630, was inducted into the Parsonage of Bemerton. He was then about thirty-six years of age.

BEMERTON CHURCH AND PARSONAGE, 1850.

Here for two years and some months he laboriously fulfilled the duties of pastor in his wide parish, which, in addition to Bemerton, included Fugglestone and Quidhampton. For these hamlets he employed a curate.

Here, too, his pen was busy, and his great work, *The Temple: Sacred Poems and Private Ejaculations,* appeared in 1631.   He wrote at this time his *Priest to the Temple,* or *Character of a Country Parson,* a prose work which was not published till 1652.   Amidst his pastoral and literary labours he yet found time to cultivate his love of music, and to go twice a week to Salisbury Cathedral for the anthem.   But, alas, tongue and pen were soon silenced and stilled.   The register of his parish contains the brief record: "Mr. George Herbert, Esq., Parson of Foughlestone and Bemerton, was buried 3 day of March, 1633."   He had lived in the spirit of his own beautiful prayer :—

> " Teach me, my God and King,
>   In all things Thee to see,
> And what I do in any thing,
>   To do it as for Thee."

His death was emphatically that of the righteous : cheered by hope, and breathing prayer and praise, his end was peace.

Shortly before or soon after Herbert's time, Bemerton was the residence of Walter Curle, who subsequently became successively Bishop of Rochester, Bath and Wells, and Winchester.   He was a prelate of great talents and most beneficent character.   The breaking out of the civil war deprived him of his preferments, and he died in needy circumstances 1647.

Sixty years after the death of Herbert, the Rectory of Bemerton was the secluded abode of another Christian poet, John Norris, of whom we shall more fully speak when we come to the place of his birth.   One anecdote of him may, however, be here told.   In the Rectory garden a grass plot slopes down to the river, commanding a fine view of Salisbury Cathedral.   Norris was there once visited by Mr. Colborne, the early friend of the poet Young.   The spire rising above the trees drew from the visitor an exclamation of surprise :—" What a magnificent structure !   You are happy, sir, in this delightful prospect."   "Yes," answered the Rector, with melancholy humour, "it is all the prospect I have with respect to that Cathedral."

The Rev.

WILLIAM COXE,

who became rector in 1788, and who was made Archdeacon of Wilts in 1805, acquired a high reputation as a traveller, historian, and antiquarian. He was the friend of Sir R. C. Hoare, whom he assisted in his great Wiltshire History. His own works were numerous. He died in 1828.

We approach *Salisbury*, the capital of the county, situated in the broad vale and bordered by pleasant downs. Three rivers—the Wiley, the Wiltshire Avon, and the intermittent Bourn, flowing through green valleys, bend their way to the city. Formerly their sparkling waters coursed, in channels bridged at numerous points, through the right-angled streets, and gained for New Sarum the name of the " English Venice." The origin of the city is not like that of the older capital, involved in the mists of antiquity, but can be distinctly traced to events which occurred in the first quarter of the thirteenth century. The disputes and strife between the soldiers of the Castle and the ecclesiastics of the Cathedral at Old Sarum, had for some time greatly interfered with the comfort and prosperity of the religious community dwelling there. In addition to this, the elevated position exposed them to storms which damaged their buildings and disturbed their services. These reasons determined Bishop Poore to seek other quarters, and being, tradition says, directed by the Virgin Mary to build in a meadow called Merrifield, he obtained an indulgence from the Pope, and in 1220 laid the foundation of that magnificent Cathedral which, with its lofty spire, stands before us, the pride of Wiltshire and the admiration of all beholders. Under the shadow of this noble building, Bishop, Dean, and Canons, with all other members of their fraternity, gathered, and a New Sarum grew up.

Historians of the city give a goodly list of eminent men who have been connected with it. One of the earliest of these was

WILLIAM LONGSPÉE, EARL OF SALISBURY,

a natural son of Henry II., by Fair Rosamond. This nobleman was famed as one of the most valiant and accomplished soldiers of his age. He was for some time engaged in military service on the Continent, and on his return had cause to accuse Hubert de Burgh of some gross enormities committed against him during his absence. The offender acknowledged his guilt, and "with great horses, and other costly gifts, obtained the Earl's favour, so that he bade the said carle to a dinner, in the which (so men thought) the earle, secretly poisoned, went to his castle at Salisbury, where he lay sick and died," in March, 1226. His burial was the first within the walls of the new Cathedral, in which an ancient monument, conjectured to be his, is still shewn.

In 1224, while the Cathedral was in building,

WALTER WINTERBURNE

was born at Salisbury. He was bred a Dominican friar, and became provincial of that order. Fuller describes him as "an excellent scholar in all studies suitable to his age when a youth, a good poet and orator when a man, and an acute philosopher when an old man." He was Confessor to Edward I., and received a Cardinal's hat from Pope Benedict XI. Visiting Rome, to pay his respects to the Pope, on the occasion of this appointment, he died at Genoa on his way home, and was buried in that city ; but his body was afterwards brought to England, and re-interred with great ceremony in London, in 1305.

WILLIAM HORMAN,

born in New Street, about 1450, became a fellow of New College, Oxford, and in 1485 was elected master of Eton College, of which he was afterwards made provost. While diligently fulfilling the duties of this station he engaged in the literary and scientific pursuits of his day, writing several works, including two on anatomy. He died in 1535, and is buried in the chapel of Eton College.

JOHN SECURIS,

another student of New College, after leaving Oxford pursued his studies at Paris, and then returning to his native county, settled at Salisbury, where he practised as a physician with great success. He published a curious sort of Almanac and also some works on his own profession. He died in 1570.

JOHN THORNBOROUGH,

born in 1552, and educated at the city free school, was successively rector of Chilmark, Dean of York, and Bishop of Limerick, 1593, Bristol, 1603, and Worcester, 1616. He wrote several works in divinity, and is reputed to have excelled as a chemist. Fuller accounts for his rapid preferment by " his goodly presence," which made him " acceptable to Queen Elizabeth." The old historian also relates that the Bishop " presented a precious extraction to King James, reputed a great preserver of health and prolonger of life." It is certain he himself lived to a great age, not dying till he was ninety-one. Fuller, however, shrewdly attributes this length of days to the influence of a " merry heart, which doeth good like a medicine," rather than to the virtues of his chemical nostrum.

GEORGE CORYAT,

who was a topographer and a Latin poet in the reign of Elizabeth, was born in the parish of St. Thomas, and educated at the free school. After going to Winchester, and Oxford he became rector of Odcombe, in Somersetshire, and subsequently prebend of Warthill, in Yorkshire. Elizabeth honoured one of his Latin works, *Descriptio Angliæ, Scotiæ, et Hiberniæ*, with her patronage. He died in 1606.

Another excellent Latin poet,

MICHAEL MASCHIART,

born here about the middle of the sixteenth century, was also an Oxford scholar. He obtained the rectory of Writtle, in Essex, where he died, 1598. He wrote several tracts and poems.

SIR TOBY MATTHEWS,

eldest son of Dr. Toby Mathews, Archbishop of York, was born at Salisbury, 1577. As a Jesuit, a politician, an ambassador, an author, and as a spy for the Pope he played many parts in the reigns of James I. and Charles I. He died in the English College of Jesuits, at Gaunt, in Flanders, 1655.

Born in the reign of Elizabeth, and contemporary with Shakespeare,

PHILIP MASSINGER

occupies a prominent place among the dramatists of that period. He was the son of a gentleman retainer of the Earl of Pembroke, and was born at Salisbury, in 1583. At eighteen he went to Oxford, but on the death of his father, four years afterwards, he removed to London, employing himself as a writer for the stage. He appears to have been on intimate terms with Shakespeare, Ben Jonson, and other poets of the time. The titles of thirty-seven of his productions are known, but only eighteen of these, of which five are tragedies, are extant. *The Duke of Milan*, and *A New Way to Pay Old Debts*, with one or two others, are the most popular; and are still occasionally placed upon the stage. Critics are divided as to the rank he should occupy. Hallam would place him second only to Shakespeare. The chief merits of his plays have been described as " unusual earnestness, religiousness of tone, and power of deep reflection." His writings, however, are not without blemishes and defilement. The poet's life, though, per- haps, more correct than those of many of his literary contemporaries, yet seems to have been one of poverty, misfortune and sadness. Its close was mysterious and lonely. On the 17th of March, 1640, he went to bed in his own house on the Bankside in good health; but was found dead next morning. He was buried in the grave of his brother dramatist Fletcher, at St. Saviour's, Southwark, where the register of deaths records :—" March

20, 1639—40, buried Philip Massinger, a stranger." New editions of his works together with memoirs of his life, continue to be published.

Aubrey says he was a servant to William, Earl of Pembroke, from whom he had a pension of twenty or thirty pounds a year ; and that this annuity continued to be paid to his wife, who after his death lived at Cardiff.

WILLIAM LAWES,

brother to Henry, whom we have already noticed at Dinton, was another of the " able musicians produced by the quire of Salisbury Cathedral." Like his brother he was private musician to Charles I., but in 1611 became chamber-musician to Prince Charles. Following the fortunes of his royal master in the civil wars, and recklessly exposing himself to danger, he was killed at the siege of Chester, 1645. The king, who deeply bewailed his death, expressed his sorrow by putting on " particular mourning" for him, though he was already in mourning for his kinsman, Lord Bernard Stuart, who was slain at the same siege.

ALEXANDER HYDE,

son of Sir Lawrence Hyde, and a native of Salisbury, was made Dean of Winchester in 1660, whence by the recommendation of his kinsman, the Earl of Clarendon, he was translated to the Bishopric of his native city in 1665. He died in August, 1667.

One of the many clergymen on both sides who suffered during the civil and religious contentions of the seventeenth century, was

JOHN EEDES,

born at Salisbury, 1609. He was educated at Oriel College, Oxford, and received a benefice in the Isle of Sheppy. On the beginning of the civil war he was ejected, and imprisoned for several months. He returned to his native city, obtained the curacy of Broadchalk, and soon afterwards became vicar of Hele. His writings gave offence to a clerical opponent, who endeavoured to injure him with the Government, but in vain. He died a violent death, his house being robbed, and himself murdered in 1667.

Another "able musician produced by the quire of Salisbury Cathedral" was

MICHAEL WISE,

a native of the city, who became Master of the Choristers and Organist of the Cathedral in 1668. Finding favour with Charles II. he was made a gentleman of the Chapel Royal in 1675. He was next appointed Almoner and Master of the Choristers of St. Paul's; but was suspended from this office, having, it is thought, offended the king by commencing the voluntary before the preacher had ended his sermon. He met with a melancholy end. Having one night in August, 1687, quarrelled with his wife, he rushed from his house, and being stopped by the watch in the street a scuffle ensued, in which he received a blow which fractured his skull and caused his death.

Among the innumerable theological writers of the same period, was

RICHARD HAYTER,

who was born 1611. He went to Oxford, and having taken a degree in arts, returned to Salisbury, where he died 1684. His chief works are on the Revelation of St. John.

JOHN GREENHILL,

as a celebrated portrait painter is justly ranked among the eminent natives of Salisbury. He was born 1640, and studied under Sir Peter Lely, showing such marked ability as to excite his master's jealousy. The portrait of Bishop Ward was one of his works. While rapidly rising into fame, he unhappily fell into habits of dissipation, and died in the prime of life, in London, 1676.

DR. THOMAS BENNETT,

who was born here in 1673, and educated at St. John's College, Cambridge, is distinguished as an able and skilful controversialist. He was especially famed for his knowledge of the Oriental and dead languages. He became rector of St. Giles, Cripplegate, London, where he died 1728.

HUMPHREY DITTON,

an eminent mathematician, was born here May 29, 1675. He entered the nonconformist ministry, and was for some time pastor of a congregation at Tunbridge. This position, however, he resigned in order to pursue his more favourite study of mathematics. Favoured with the friendship and interest of Sir Isaac Newton, he obtained the appointment of master of the Mathematical School, Christ's Hospital, where he continued till his death, 1715. In addition to various works on mathematics, he published a discourse on the *Resurrection of Jesus*.

On the south side of the Avon, and connected with Salisbury by a bridge, is *Harnham*, forming one of the pleasant suburbs of the city. Here, in 1679, was born

THOMAS CHUBB,

who acquired much notoriety as a controversial writer on moral and theological questions. His father was a glover, but Thomas preferred the work of a tallow chandler, in which he was employed for several years. He gave his mind to the pursuit of knowledge, and particularly to the study of divinity. In 1715 he wrote a work on the Trinity, under the title of *The Supremacy of the Father Asserted*, which excited great attention, and brought him into acquaintance with several men of rank and genius. Encouraged by this success he continued to direct his thoughts to these subjects, and published several works chiefly of a controversial character, and all more or less impugning the orthodox views. Notwithstanding his popularity as a writer, and his friendship with many distinguished men, Chubb sought no change of circumstances, but continued to live in the pursuit of his calling, and died in 1747, at the age of 68. He was an attendant at church, but his works, especially some published after his death, indicate a strong tendency to deism.

The present Earl of Malmesbury is descended from

JAMES HARRIS,

the author of *Hermes*, a philological and philosophical writer of repute, who was born at Salisbury in 1709. He was trained in the law, but succeeding to an independent fortune he gave himself to the more congenial pursuits of philosophy and classical learning. He also gave some attention to politics, and was elected for Christchurch in 1761. Shortly afterwards he was made a Lord of the Admiralty, and in 1763 was promoted a Lord of the Treasury. He died in 1780. His son was created Earl of Malmesbury in 1800.

DR. WILLIAM HARRIS,

a Nonconformist minister, eminent as a writer of history and biography, was born 1720. He was successively pastor of congregations at St Looe in Cornwall, Wells, and Luppit near Honiton, where he died 1770. Among other works he wrote *Historical and Critical Accounts of the Lives of James I., Charles I., Oliver Cromwell,* and *Charles II.,* the spirit and style of which have been greatly admired.

A successor to Massinger appeared in

JOHN TOBIN,

who was born at Salisbury in 1770. He was articled to a solicitor of Lincoln's Inn, and afterwards became member of a legal firm. Influenced by an intense love of the drama, he devoted his hours of repose and relaxation to dramatic study and composition. His health suffering from incessant application to professional and literary pursuits, he was advised by his physicians to go on a voyage to the West Indies. Disease had, however, gone too far, and a few days after the ship had sailed from Bristol he expired. His drama of *The Honeymoon* has been much admired. *The Curfew*, for the copyright of which Sir Richard Phillips gave £400, is considered in some respects superior to it.

DR. RICHARD FOWLER,

who died at Milford April 18, 1863, in the 98th year of his age, had passed 67 years of his long life at Salisbury. The eminent professional abilities of this distinguished physician, and his numerous writings on various scientific subjects obtained for him a wide celebrity. As a member of several learned societies he originated discussions on many important questions, and gave an impetus to investigations which have led to valuable results. During his long life he was on friendly terms with most of the leading political, literary and scientific men of his time ; and was specially intimate with the Marquis of Lansdowne, Lord Holland, the poet Bowles, and Lord Herbert of Lea.

To this list of Salisbury worthies the citizens with one consent would add the name of

EDWARD THOMAS STEVENS,

whose life closed as recently as August 18, 1878. This gentleman, belonging to an ancient family of the city, acquired great repute as a most intelligent and enterprising geologist and archæologist. His researches were carried on not only in his own county, but in various parts of England and also of the Continent: and served to throw much light upon the enigmas of pre-historic periods. To the stone, bronze, and early iron remains of those remote ages he devoted much time and study. In these pursuits he became intimately associated with Sir John Lubbock, Sir Charles Lyell, and other distinguished scientific and literary men. His writings, while affording proof of the great care and industry with which his inquiries had been pursued, were also marked by considerable literary skill, and secured him a place in the front rank of English writers on these subjects. Referring to his death, at the comparatively early age of fifty, the *Salisbury and Winchester Journal*, in an article from which the foregoing brief particulars have been gathered, said, " He dies sincerely regretted and esteemed by all classes ; and we cannot but feel that by his departure from among us archæology has lost a diligent student, science a devoted pioneer, and the city of Salisbury a gentleman of great culture, refinement, and courtesy, who was in force of intellect and general knowledge second to none amongst our fellow citizens."

Leaving Salisbury for the present, and moving towards the upper part of the county, we come to *Stratford-under-the-Castle*, lying on the east bank of the Avon, about two miles north-west. It was at one time the residence of the Pitt family, and it has been asserted that the great Earl Chatham was born in the old family mansion here. This is more than doubtful, but it is certain that his father, Robert Pitt, Esq., lived here, and that he himself commenced his Parliamentary career as representative for Old Sarum under circumstances which Macaulay thus relates :—" At the general election of 1734 his elder brother Thomas was chosen both for Old Sarum and Oakhampton. When Parliament met in 1735 Thomas made his election to serve for Oakhampton, and William was returned for Old Sarum."

Old Sarum, situated in this parish, is a place of great antiquarian interest and political notoriety. It is now a vast mound, partly under cultivation and partly in a state of nature, but was for centuries the site of one of the chief places in the kingdom. Long after it had become almost utterly depopulated it retained the right of returning two members to Parliament, but was disfranchised by the Reform Bill of 1832. Within two or three furlongs of the parish church is a tree under which the election of members for this remarkable borough took place.

JOHN OF SALISBURY,

a man of considerable learning, was born here about 1120. He was a fellow pupil with Thomas à Becket, and afterwards tutor to young noblemen. Being made a clerk at Canterbury he obtained the favour of Theobald, the Archbishop, and was appointed his secretary. His old fellow scholar Beckett succeeded Theobald, and retained John as his secretary. He was a devoted follower of this lordly primate, and narrowly escaped sharing his fate at the time of his assassination. In 1176 Henry II. made him Bishop of Chartres in France, where he died four or five years afterwards. He wrote several works, one of which, *On the Trifles of the Courtiers and Tracks of the Philosophers*, contains some remarkable features, particularly that of an elaborate argument for tyrannicide under the direction and authority of the Church ! Fuller gives us ' a tast' of the pungency with which, ecclesiastic though he was, he rebuked " the pride and covetousness of the Court of Rome." " Scribes and Pharisees," he wrote, " sit in the Church of Rome, putting unbearable burthens on men's backs. His Legates do so swagger, as if Satan were gone forth from the face of the Lord to scourge the Church. They eat the sins of the people, with them they are clothed, and many ways riot therein, whilst the true worshippers worship the Father in Spirit. Whoso dissent from their doctrines are condemed for hereticks or schismaticks. Christ therefore will manifest himself, and make the way plain wherein we should walk." In spirit and in style he seems to have been a forerunner of Wycliffe and Tyndale.

Still moving north-west we reach *Steeple Langford*, a village on the banks of the Wiley, of which

THOMAS MARRIOTT,

a divine and author, was a native. He became fellow of New College, Oxford, in 1610, and afterwards vicar of Swalclive, near Banbury. Engaging in tuition he wrote two school books, one called *Vulgaria*, a collection of common phrases ; the other *Adagia Selectissima*, a selection of proverbs. He died in 1662, and was buried in his own church.

Mr. Robert Benson, in his Memoirs of the Life and Writings of

ARTHUR COLLIER,

rector of Steeple Langford, makes us acquainted with a remarkable member of a remarkable family. Joseph Collier, of whom there is a monumental effigy in the church, was presented to the rectory in 1608. Henry Collier, his son and successor, appears to have suffered severely during the Commonwealth, being ejected from his house and with his wife and eleven children turned into the street in a deep snow. At the Restoration he was reinstated in his parsonage, which he held till his death in 1672. He was succeeded by his son Arthur, who in turn was followed by his son, the subject of this sketch, who was born October 12, 1680, and bore his father's name. He entered Pembroke College, Oxford, in 1697, in which year his father died : the following year he and his brother became students of Baliol. In 1704 he was instituted on the presentation of his mother to the living of his native parish, and thus became the fourth of the family who had had the rectory. Here he continued till his death in 1732. The Recreations of this Country Parson consisted chiefly of metaphysical pursuits. He deeply studied the works of ancient and modern philosophers, and appears to have been greatly influenced by the opinions of John Norris, of Bemerton. He corresponded with most of the great metaphysicians of his day ; and also worked diligently in elaborating and expounding his own views. These were made known in a work published in 1713, entitled *Clavis Universalis; or a New Inquiry after Truth, being a Demonstration of the Non-Existence or Impossibility of an External World.* His conclusions were similar to those of Bishop Berkeley; and the depth and ingenuity of his reasoning found many admirers among philosophical authorities both in England and Germany. He left several unpublished MSS. His brother William, who was rector of Baverstock, appears to have pursued the same studies as himself, and though not equalling him as a metaphysician, surpassed him as a writer. One of Arthur's daughters—Jane—was the authoress of a clever work *The Art of Ingeniously Tormenting.*

Four miles north-east of Langford is the parish of *Wilsford,* including *Lake.* The following admirable sketch of the late Rev.

EDWARD DUKE, M.A.,

of Lake House, has been kindly supplied by Mr. W. C. Kemm, of Amesbury :—

Passing from Amesbury down the Avon vale by West Amesbury, along a pleasant road by the side of the water meadows, a short three miles brings us to the picturesque domain of Lake, with its fine Elizabethan Manor House, probably erected by George Duke, Esquire, who purchased the estate in 1578. There is, however, reason to believe that there were some of that family and name resident at Lake before that time. From the above-named ancestor the estate passed down to the late Rev. Edward Duke, M.A., than whom none could be more worthy to possess or better able to appreciate such a fine and interesting relic of olden time.

He succeeded to the property in 1805, and resided there from that period till his decease. The late Mr. Duke was born at Hungerford, Berks, just on the border of Wilts, in the year 1779. He was the representative of the ancient family of Duke, settled originally at Power Hayes, Devon, and subsequently at Otterton, in that county, and descended from common ancestors with the great Earl of Clarendon, and from the once powerful and distinguished Hungerford family. His long residence at Lake, as well as such a Wiltshire ancestry, fully warrants us in claiming him as one of the worthies of the county, among the foremost of whom he deserves a place. A worthy he truly was, and not merely a celebrity. Soon after succeeding to the family property at Lake he was honoured with the friendship of that accomplished antiquary, Sir R. C. Hoare, in whose company he proceeded to investigate the contents of the tumuli on his estate. Various articles, the produce of their joint labours, are described and figured by Sir R. C. Hoare, in his " Ancient Wiltshire," and are now preserved in the museum at Lake House.

Mr. Duke was for some years a frequent contributor to the " Gentleman's Magazine." Letters from his pen are to be found in most of its volumes between 1823 and 1828. They mostly relate to the antiquities of his county; the latest of them contains his matured theory on Stonehenge, and is in the number for December, 1849. Contributions from him also may be found in the volumes entitled " Ancient Reliques," and perhaps some other antiquarian miscellanies.

In 1837 Mr. Duke published a volume entitled " Prolusiones Historicæ ; or Essays Illustrative of the Halle of John Halle, Citizen and Merchant of Salisbury, in the Reigns of Henry VI. and Edward IV.," a learned and most highly interesting book to every Wiltshire archæologist, and little less so to archæologists in general. This was followed a few years later by the publication of " The Druidical Temples of Wilts," in which work was developed the theory that the very early inhabitants of this part of our island had " pourtrayed a vast planetarium or stationary orrery on the face of the Wiltshire Downs," the earth being represented by Silbury Hill, and the sun and planets revolving round it by seven temples, four of stone and three of earth, located at their proper distances on a meridional line thirty-two miles in extent. In the autumn of 1849, when the Archæological Institute held its meeting at Salisbury, the same hand contributed a paper on Stonehenge, which was printed in the volume of that body relating to Wiltshire.

Mr. Duke was long one of the most active magistrates in the county of Wilts, and chairman of one of its Courts of Quarter Sessions. His conduct in the fulfilment of those duties was peculiarly fearless and uncompromising, and most strictly upright and impartial. He was also an attentive *ex-officio* guardian of the poor, to whose claims he ever gave the most fair and just consideration. Such conduct, of course, at times raised him up opponents, but none could ever impugn the honesty and goodness of his intentions, or impute to him any but the best of motives.

As a clergyman, though unbeneficed, he was ever willing to take clerical duty when a neighbour required help, and he was a faithful upholder of the principles of the Reformation.

It scarcely needs be said that as a man of learning and an antiquary Mr. Duke held a high position. He was a Fellow of the Antiquarian and Linnean Societies. His mental habits were marked by much industry and vigour. He was continually occupied, and even the pain and lassitude of sickness had no power to divorce him from his favourite studies. After a day of business or social intercourse, he often returned to his studies and continued them far into the night. His reading embraced a wide range of subjects. He posessed much legal knowledge, and was familiar with the best works on the various branches of natural history. The acquisitions made by his industry he was enabled to retain by the power of a memory retentive to an uncommon degree. He possessed a valuable library, and for many years was at much pains and expense in collecting every Wiltshire author he could obtain. Amidst all his acquirements, however, he ever looked with favour on and gave encouragement to the humblest of those who were attached to similar pursuits.

Mr. Duke married in 1819, Harriet, daughter of Henry Hinxman, Esq., of Ivy Church, near Salisbury, by whom he had issue four sons and four daughters. He is succeeded by his eldest son of the same name, who is also in holy orders, and who has recently published a very interesting work entitled "Beneath the Surface, or Physical Truths Latent in the Holy Scriptures."

Salisbury Plain is now before us. The term "Romantic Wiltshire"

H

applies more fitly to the vast plains and downs than to any portion of the county. Across their length and breadth romance is written as fully as upon any of the forests or mountains of the kingdom. It is easy for the imagination to fill each wide expanse with manifold scenes, and people it with a variety of life. Barrows, encampments, stones, roads, and footways are eloquent of the past, and discourse of pre-historic times and races as well as of events of every period of our own national history. Well nigh every acre might tell some tale which would form a subject for the painter or the poet. Funeral pomps, religious solemnities, military pageants, battles, murders, robberies, wild sports, and tender love scenes, shepherds perishing with their flocks in the fierce winter tempest, and benighted travellers sleeping the sleep of death in the wild snow drift, are all inwrought in the written and unwritten annals of these ancient wastes. The spacious plain is, however, far from being either a dead level or a solitary desert. Gentle elevations assuming the form of rounded knolls or ranging for short distances as connected ridges, rise in all directions. It is indented, too, by numerous valleys where little villages and hamlets lie sheltered, and through which streamlets flow.

The one spot to which, more than to any other, the thoughts turn, and around which the most mysterious interest gathers, is where Stonehenge, "that wondrous pyle of rugged mountaynes standes,"

"The noblest monument of Albion's isle."

A walk of about two miles northward from Wilsford brings us to "the great stones," of which many descriptions have been given. Nothing, however, but a visit will afford the mind an adequate impression of the strange scene. The more lonely and leisurely the visit is, the more likely is the impression to be true and lasting. If it can be made at early dawn amidst the glories of sun-rising, or can be extended through the shades of evening or into hours of moonlight, so much the better.

Two miles east of this solitary and sublime ruin is the little town of Amesbury, a prettily situated place in the valley of the Avon, of more than 1000 inhabitants, and possessing many features of archæological interest.

Among the abbots of Glastonbury the name of

MICHAEL OF AMESBURY,

most probably a native of this parish, deservedly holds a distinguished place. Succeeding Abbot Robert in 1234, he zealously set himself to restore the prosperity of the Abbey, which had suffered both in Spirituals and Temporals. His energy was untiring and his labours abundant, so that alienated possessions were recovered, lost rights regained, debts discharged, the lands diligently cultivated, and the Abbey well provided with cattle, sheep, and agricultural produce, as well as enriched with plate, money, and other effects. As a spiritual ruler he was also diligent and exemplary. He is said to have loved and cherished the brethren, and to have well governed the Church and ordered the house and himself. "He was diligent in instructing the young, modest and meek in reproving and correcting; always free from reproaches, hard words, or austerity." After eighteen years of activity he resigned his office and sought retirement, but died the following year, 1253.

Other natives and notable residents have honourable mention in the traditions and annals of this interesting little town. One of these,

JOHN ROSE,

when a boy, left Amesbury to seek employment in London. We next hear of him on the title page of a book published in the reign of Charles II., which reads thus :—*The English Vineyard Vindicated ; By John Rose, Gardiner to His Majesty at his Royal Garden in St. James's, Formerly Gardiner to Her Grace the Duchess of Somerset. With an address where the best plants are to be had at easie rates.* The work originated in a conversation between Rose and the celebrated John Evelyn ; and it appears that while the former supplied the information the latter prepared it for publication. Rose was the first to cultivate the pine-apple in England, and a painting representing his presentation of the delicious fruit to the king adorned the royal residence. He died Sept. 17, 1677, and was buried in the church of St. Martin's-in-the-Fields. In his prosperity he did not forget his native town. The bulk of his property was bequeathed to the parish of Amesbury. Part was devoted to the maintenance of a Free Grammar School for twenty boys, one of the first scholars in which was Joseph Addison. Twenty pounds were applied to the purchase of communion plate for the church on some of which his name appears.

A contrivance for throwing grain for the action of the fan in the winnowing machine, and known as the Amesbury Heaver, was the invention of

JOHN TROWBRIDGE

a native of this parish. He was a man in humble circumstances, but possessed an inventive and useful genius. He was one of the earliest, if not the first, to apply the loom to the weaving of wire for winnowing and other purposes. He died in 1823.

The relation of Amesbury to Stonehenge is ancient and intimate; and the inhabitants of the little town naturally feel a deep interest in the mysterious ruin of which by near neighbourhood they seem constituted the custodians.

Visiting Amesbury in 1822 for the purpose of delivering a course of lectures on ancient history

HENRY BROWNE,

a gentleman of Worcester, had his attention strongly drawn to these wonderful remains. Taking up his residence in the town he pursued his archæological researches on the Plain with great ardour. Pen and pencil, pickaxe and spade were all employed in the prosecution of his work. With much ingenuity and exactness he constructed, chiefly while on the spot and with few mechanical aids, a model of Stonehenge for himself; and then proceeded to make a second which when complete he placed upon a sort of wheelbarrow and early one morning set out with it for London. "After a toilsome and almost continuous march of two days and nights, (for he only slept a short time in the day) he arrived on the morning of the third day at the British Museum, showed a letter he had got from the Trustees to the porter, wheeled his load into the courtyard, and saw his model safely deposited in the house. He left without staying to be questioned, and was soon on his way home again; but was detained for some days on the road by illness brought on by his exertions."

He continued his pursuits as a lecturer for many years, and also published several pamphlets on various subjects—including one on Stonehenge and Abury. Like many other active and inquiring minds Mr. Browne essayed to explore the mysteries of the Apocalypse. The results of his studies were given to the public in two or three pamphlets, which like most works on the same subject have passed into oblivion. His death resulting from over exertion in a long walk to fulfil a lecturing engagement at Winchester occurred in that city April 17, 1839; and he lies buried in Amesbury Churchyard. Mr. Browne was uncle to the popular authoress--" Charlotte Elizabeth." His son

JOSEPH HENRY BICKERTON BROWNE,

like himself felt the charm of Stonehenge, and for more than forty years devoted himself to illustrating it by models and drawings; and acting as guide to visitors. He passed so much time on the spot, both by night and day, as to seem almost a portion of the same. His presence served to protect the ruin from injury and defilement, and the information which he intelligently and courteously afforded to strangers was highly appreciated. When at length compelled to relinquish attendance through infirmity, the kindness of friends enabled him to live in retirement till his death on 26 Feb., 1881, at the age of 84.

The annals of Amesbury Manor would form a long and interesting chapter in Wiltshire History. The Abbey which occupied the site of the present residence of Sir Edmund Antrobus, Bart., M.P., originated in a nunnery founded by Elfrida in atonement for the murder of her son-in-law Edward the Martyr. Many distinguished names are found in its records. Eleanor the widowed Queen of Henry III., the Princess Mary daughter of Edward I., and at least thirteen ladies of noble birth, were at one time numbered among its sisterhood. It was surrendered at the dissolution in 1540, and shortly afterwards granted to Sir Edward Seymour. It was next carried by marriage into the family of Bruce Earls of Aylesbury; and in 1720 was sold by Lord Charles Bruce to Lord

Carleton, by whom it was left five years afterwards to his nephew Charles, third Duke of Queensberry. This nobleman and his Duchess, Katherine Hyde, daughter of Henry Earl of Clarendon, were the patrons and friends of the poet Gay, who is said to have here written some of his best pieces and passed some of the happiest years of his life. After some changes of owners the estate was sold to Sir Edmund Antrobus, Bart., in 1824, who on his death in 1826 was succeeded by his nephew, the second baronet of that name. The term of his proprietorship was one of sunshine to the people of Amesbury. He rebuilt the Abbey, as the Manor House is called, restored the Church, and spent large sums in building and planting on the property. He died May 4, 1870, "leaving a blessed memory."

Orcheston St. Mary, a few miles north-west across the Plain from Stonehenge, is noted for some remarkable grass, of which wonderful tales have been told. The astonishing fertility of the meadow in which it flourishes appears from the statements of Dr. Maton and others who assure us that the grass reaches the length of seven feet and upwards ; and that two and a half acres have yielded 12 tons of exceedingly nutritive hay in one season.

Four miles north is the little village of *Netheravon*. "When first I went into the Church," says Sidney Smith, "I had a curacy in the middle of Salisbury Plain." It was here that the witty parson was located, and for the space of two years suffered, according to Lady Holland's humorous account, grievous mental and bodily privations. "Once a week," she writes, "a butcher's cart came over from Salisbury, it was then only that he could obtain any meat, and he often dined on a mess of potatoes sprinkled with a little ketchup. Too poor to command books, his only resource was the squire, and his only relaxation long walks over these interminable plains, in one of which he narrowly escaped being buried in a snow drift."

Hazlitt, another sojourner on the Plain, records pleasanter experiences. In his *Lectures on the Drama* he says, "Here, on Salisbury Plain, where I write this, even here with a few old authors I can manage to get through the winter or the summer months without ever knowing what it is to feel *ennui*. They sit with me at breakfast, they walk with me before dinner. After a long walk through unfrequented tracts, after starting the hare from the fern, or hearing the wing of the raven over my head, or being greeted with the woodman's 'good night' as he strikes into his narrow homeward path, I can take mine ease at mine inn beside the blazing hearth, and shake hands with Signor Orlando Frescobaldo as the oldest acquaintance I have. Ben Jonson, learned Chapman, Master Webster, and Master Heywood are there, and seated round discourse the silent hours away."

Another pleasurable reminiscence is beautifully told by the same charming writer. " I remember," he says, " once strolling along the margin of a stream, in one of those long sheltered valleys on Salisbury Plain, where the monks of former ages had planted chapels and built hermits' cells. There was a little parish church near ; but tall elms and quivering alders hid it from the sight, when, all on a sudden, I was startled by the sound of the full organ pealing on the ear, accompanied by rustic voices and the willing choir of village maids and children. It rose, indeed, 'like an exhalation of rich distilled perfumes.' The dew from a thousand pastures was gathered in its softness—the silence of a thousand years spoke in it. It came upon the heart like the calm beauty of death ; fancy caught the sound, and faith mounted on it to the skies. It filled the valley like a mist, and still poured out its endless chant, and still it swells upon the ear, and wraps me in a golden trance, drowning the noisy tumult of the world."

PART IV.

MID WILTS.—*NORTH*.

" So brief our existence, a glimpse, at the most,
    Is all we can have of the few we hold dear;
And oft even joy is unheeded and lost,
    For want of some heart, that would echo it, near.
Ah, well may we hope, when this short life is gone,
    To meet in some world of more permanent bliss;
For a smile, or a grasp of the hand, hastening on,
    Is all we enjoy of each other in this."
                                                        MOORE.

THE Parliamentary division line crosses the Plain from a little south of Upavon on the east side to a little south of Imber on the west, thus passing south of Black Heath. Of the road crossing this line from Lavington to Chittern a writer in the Wiltshire Magazine for 1867 tells a tale which may serve as a caution to late-houred Leanders.

" Some years ago a gentleman residing at Chittern paid his addresses to a very fascinating young lady at Lavington, whose attractions were frequently the cause of his having to cross the downs at a very late hour. On one of these occasions, being unusually late, he found that though ' the course of true love' was in his case tolerably *smooth*, it was by no means *straight,* for after wandering about during the whole of a most miserable night, he found himself in the morning only a mile or two from the place whence he had set out on the previous evening. To prevent the recurrence of a similar misfortune, he had a quantity of chalk placed at such distances, as that even in the darkest night it would be easy to trace his way across this grassy Hellespont in safety." These landmarks are now jocularly termed " Wiltshire lanterns." Memorials of other strange, and more tragic, incidents are found here and there on the Plain. We scarcely cross the line before we come on one near a spot formerly known as John a Gore's Cross. About forty years ago a Mr. Deane, of Imber, in returning from Devizes was attacked and robbed by three foot-pads at Gore Cross. Some friends who heard his cries for assistance joined him in pursuit of the robbers, one of whom, in his desperate efforts to escape, fell dead on a spot now marked by a stone.

Lineal descendants of the primate, Thomas à Becket, were long connected with the parish of *West* or *Bishop Lavington*. A slab in the handsome parish church records the death of Thomas à Becket, of Littleton Pannell, Feb. 1, 1792. The residence of the Becket family was the scene of a barbarous murder during the civil war, in December, 1644. The victim, Captain Henry Penruddocke, was a royalist officer. The crime, which was committed by some of Ludlow's troopers, was marked by revolting cruelty; and was doubtless as deeply deplored and condemned by the high-souled republican General as by any of the young Captain's own partizans. The circumstances are thus told by a newspaper of the time:

" Finding young Mr. Penruddocke (second son of Sir John Penruddocke, late Sheriff of the county), in one of the rooms where he had fallen asleep in a chair, after two nights of hard service, they pulled him by the hair, knocked him down, and broke two pistols over his head, without so much as tendering him quarter. The gentlewoman of the house and her two daughters then fell upon their knees before the soldiers, begging for the life of their guest, declaring that he was a gentleman, and whose son he was, upon which one of the troopers, who was a collier, swore that he should die for his father's sake, and putting a pistol to his belly, shot him dead."

Colonel John Penruddocke, the elder brother of this unfortunate young officer, also met a tragic end, being beheaded at Exeter in April, 1655, for an attempt to overturn Cromwell's government. Hugh Grove, of Chisenbury, in the parish of Enford, was executed at the same time.

Few Wiltshire characters are more widely known, and few have obtained greater popularity than Hannah More's *Shepherd of Salisbury Plain*. We can scarcely tread the great plain with its shepherds and flocks without some recollections of his homely figure and cheerful face, while many of his quaint and pious sayings are recalled by the scenes which the amiable authoress has rendered familiar to our minds. He was not, as some have supposed, simply a creation of good Hannah's lively imagination, but a character drawn from real life, bearing the name of

DAVID SAUNDERS,

and living somewhere in this parish. The origin of the tract is related by Mr. Jay who, at a breakfast party at Mrs. More's house, was requested to read the manuscript for the criticism of the company. "This I did," he says, "but not without difficulty, being affected to tears with some of its exquisite touches." Of the shepherd himself a writer in the Evangelical Magazine for 1805, says "though simple and unlearned as the world would call him he possessed uncommon natural abilities ; and, what is far better, was endued with a large portion of that wisdom which is from above, pure and peaceable." The same writer assures us that the tract "contains a just delineation of this extraordinary person ;" and that "the conversations recited are in perfect harmony with his character." Sir James Stonhouse, an eminent physician who entered the church and became rector of *Cheveril*, has also communicated some interesting particulars concerning him. A paragraph in a London newspaper of Sept. 15th, 1796, thus records his death :—"Last week at Wyke [Wick], between Bath and Bristol, in the seventieth year of his age, David Saunders, of West Lavington, Wilts, whose distinguished piety and moral excellence furnished Miss H. More with materials for her much admired story of "The Shepherd of Salisbury Plain."

The churchyard is the resting place of the Rev.

EDWARD WILTON,

who was sometime minister of the Chapelry of Earl Stoke ; and from 1832 till 1871 Master of West Lavington Endowed School. Mr. Wilton, who was born at Edington, near Trowbridge, in 1797, was a student of Queen's College, Oxford. He was known as "an accurate and persevering archæologist, and a complete master in heraldry." For some time he was a contributor to the original *Gentleman's Magazine ;* and afterwards to the more modern *Notes and Queries*. He died May 4, 1871. A paper on Bishop Tanner, one of his latest productions, appeared in Vol. XIII. of the Wiltshire Magazine.

The pleasantly situated town of *East* or *Market Lavington*, lying in a green valley at the foot of chalk hills, was the birthplace of

DR. THOMAS TANNER,

who was the son of the vicar of the parish, and was born in 1674. This learned and laborious writer was an eminent antiquary and the author of some valuable works. He was educated at Queen's College, Cambridge, " a college then selected by Wiltshire men as affording special advantages to natives of that county in appropriated Scholarships and Fellowships." Having entered holy orders when twenty years of age, he soon obtained preferment, and in 1731 was consecrated Bishop of St. Asaph's, a dignity he did not long enjoy, as he died Dec. 14, 1735. His chief work entitled *Notitia Monastica; or a Short Notice of the Religious Houses in England and Wales*, was published in 1695; and was compiled when he was "scarce twenty years old." Among the numerous manuscripts he left were some memoranda for a history of his native county. He bequeathed £200 to his native town, directing the interest to be expended as follows : To the Vicar or Curate for a sermon on some practical subject, to be preached on the Conversion Day of St. Paul, 13s. 4d. ; Clerk and Sexton for attending and ringing the bell, 3s. ; Ringers for two short peals, one at break of day and another after afternoon service, 6s. ; Friendly meeting in evening to promote peace and good neighbourhood, 20s. ; Teaching of poor children to read and write, 20s. ; To buy 4 Bibles with Common Prayer for 4 poor persons, 20s. ; and the remainder to be distributed " to poor persons at 12 pence each."

Fifty years ago a Wiltshire farmer,

HENRY HUNT,

was one of the most active and popular political characters in the kingdom. In person, career, and character he was a remarkable man. Born at Widdington Farm, in the parish of *Upavon*, in 1773, he was bred to agriculture; and successfully farmed a large quantity of land at *Enford*, regularly attending Devizes market. In 1795 he married Miss Halcombe, of the Bear Inn, in that town. As evidence of his prosperity it is related that " in the year 1801, when the apprehension of an invasion was so great that the Lord Lieutenant of the county caused letters to be written to the churchwardens, requiring from every parish a return of all moveable property, live and dead stock, &c., in Mr. Hunt's schedule were enumerated:— wheat, 1600 sacks; barley, 1500 quarters; oats, 400 qrs.; hay, 250 tons; cart horses, 30, value from 30 to 70 guineas each; working oxen, 10; cows, 20; sheep, 4,200, &c.; altogether valued at £20,000." As proof of his patriotism it should be added that " the whole of this property he voluntarily tendered to the Government to be at their service in case of an invasion. He also engaged to enter himself and three servants, completely equipped and mounted upon valuable hunters, as volunteers into the regiment of horse that should make the first charge upon the enemy." This offer was talked of all through the country, and the patriotic farmer received the thanks of the Lord Lieutenant.

Some time after, in consequence of a misunderstanding, he received a letter from Lord Bruce, saying that his services in the Marlborough troop of yeomanry cavalry would be no longer required, and requesting him to return his sword and pistols by the bearer. The high spirited yeoman, more disposed to use his weapons than to deliver them up, answered in person, and demanded satisfaction. For this offence he was fined £100 and imprisoned six weeks! In prison his political sentiments were greatly influenced by some early Radicals whom he met there, and from that time he began a new course. In 1812 he and Cobbett were unsuccessful candidates for Parliamentary honours at Bristol. He also twice contested the county of Somerset without success. His popularity was, nevertheless, very great, and " Orator Hunt," as he was commonly called, was unrivalled in his sway over the vast masses he was accustomed to attract and harangue. He was chairman and chief speaker in the assembly of 80,000 people near Manchester when the " Peterloo massacre" was perpetrated by the authorities in August, 1819. Hunt, who was arrested and imprisoned, received wide public sympathy, and when the term of his imprisonment expired he was welcomed to London by the largest concourse ever gathered in England.

At length he entered Parliament as member for Preston 1830, and was re-elected in 1831, but lost his seat the following year, and died at the age of 62 on February 13th, 1835.

In personal appearance he was considered the finest man in the House of Commons, being "tall, muscular, with a healthful sun-tinged florid complexion, and a manly deportment—half yeoman, half sportsman." While living on his farm he generally drove to Devizes market four-in-hand; and such was his skill and strength that he was able to do a day's work with any labourer in the country. Numerous anecdotes are told of the labours of "this modern Hercules."

His education was imperfect; his information often only slight and one-sided; and readiness rather than strength was the characteristic of his understanding. Many, however, of what were considered his extreme views have been embodied in subsequent legislation.

In 1730 the Rev. Joseph Spence, Professor of Poetry at Oxford, introduced to the public

STEPHEN DUCK

as "a poet from the barn." Duck, who was at that time a thresher, was a native of *Great Charlton*, a mile or so north of Upavon, where he was born of poor parents, and received but little education. At fourteen he became a farm servant, but found time and opportunities for self-improvement. Reading Milton's *Paradise Lost* his religious feelings and poetical faculties were quickened, and he began to write verse. His compositions attracted favourable attention, and his friends obtained for him a pension of £30 a year from Queen Caroline. He now studied for the Church, and was presented with the rectory of Byfleet in Surrey. His chief works, *The Thresher's Labour*, *The Shunamite*, and some others, were published in a quarto volume and had a good sale. Duck, who appears to have been a man of amiable and retiring disposition, fell into religious melancholy, under the influence of which he drowned himself at Reading in 1756.

Britton writing in 1801, says "the late Lord Palmerston purchased an acre of land at Rushall, the adjoining parish to Charlton, and ordered the rent to be appropriated, for ever, to the purchase of a dinner and strong beer for the threshers of Charlton, to be given at the Red Lion Inn, in that village, in order to preserve the memory of the unfortunate bard. The land is let at a guinea per annum ; and the dinner given on the 30th of June in every succeeding summer."

The road from Charlton to Devizes passes *Conock*, a hamlet in the parish of *Chirton* or *Cherington*, standing pretty nearly in the centre of the shire, about five miles south-east from Devizes. Situated so near the middle of the county, lying on the highway between London and Bath and Bristol, an ancient Parliamentary borough and a market and assize town, Devizes has ever been a place of great importance in the shire, and occupied the position of a secondary capital. It stands on a sort of table land of large extent, and of considerable elevation, being 500 feet above the level of the sea. Its origin is remote and uncertain, and there are but scant materials for its early history. A castle of great strength built by Roger, Bishop of Salisbury, in the time of Henry I., was the scene of some occurrences of importance ; but has long since disappeared. Many events of interest are recorded in the annals of the town ; and its history is not without some names of note. One of these is that of

RICHARD OF THE DEVIZES,

a Benedictine Friar, who lived in the twelfth century, and acquired great distinction by his learning. He wrote a history of the reign of Richard I., and other works, and died about the year 1200.

DR. THOMAS PIERCE,

who was appointed to the Deanery of Sarum May 4, 1675, was a son of John Pierce, of " The Devizes." He was a Fellow of Magdalen College, Oxford, but was ejected by the Parliamentary Visitors in 1648, on suspicion of having written a satire upon them. He received a recompense at the Restoration, being made Prebendary at Lincoln and also at Canterbury ; besides holding the rectory of Brington in Northamptonshire. The following year he became President of his own College, a post which he resigned the year in which he obtained the Deanery. He was a poet, preacher, controversialist, and author of some note. He published several works; one of which was in angry controversy with his diocesan—Bishop Seth Ward—in opposition to some of that prelate's claims. In this contention the Dean was worsted, and had to make his submission to the Bishop. He died at North Tidworth May 28, 1691, and was there buried. Mr. W. C. Kemm says—"There is a fragment of Pierce's tomb in North Tidworth Churchyard. It had once a canopy which has entirely disappeared: the clerk told Mr. Edwards and me that the stone was used for some repair of the Church!"

The celebration of the Sunday School centenary brought the name of the saintly

JOSEPH ALLEINE

into fresh prominence. This eminent Nonconformist minister was the son of Mr. Tobias Alleine, and was born in the house now occupied by the Misses Penstone and Hallett, in the Market Place, in 1633. He was sent at the age of sixteen to Lincoln College, Oxford, from whence he removed to Corpus Christi College, in 1651, on a Wiltshire scholarship. At the age of twenty-two he became assistant in the ministry to Mr. Newton, of Taunton, where he remained till ejected for Nonconformity on Bartholomew's Day, 1662. Continuing to preach, he was thrown into Ilchester gaol, and being tried at the Assizes, was fined 100 marks and to remain in prison till this large sum was paid. He suffered more than a year's confinement, during which his health was greatly injured. His zeal remained unabated, and on his release he not only continued preaching, but engaged in those efforts for the instruction of the young which have given his name a place among the earliest originators of Sunday Schools. He was again imprisoned for three months, and left the gaol in a sadly enfeebled condition; but he again resumed his labours of love, though obliged to move about on crutches, or be carried from place to place. In 1666 he visited his native place for the benefit of his health, but his self-sacrificing life closed at Bath, in 1668. He was buried in the church of St. Magdalen, at Taunton, his gravestone bearing the following inscription :—

"Here Mr. Joseph Alleine lies,
To God and you a sacrifice."

One of his works, *An Alarm to the Unconverted*, has passed through several editions. Dr. Stanford, by his well written book *Joseph Alleine: His Companions and Times*, has done much to preserve the memory of this excellent man.

DR. PHILIP STEPHENS,

also born here in the first part of the seventeenth century, was educated for the profession of medicine at St. Albans Hall, Oxford. He was elected Fellow of New College, in 1655, whence he was translated as principal to Hart Hall. He was joint author with Mr. Brown of a work entitled *Catalogus Horti Botanici Oxonienses*, which was published in 1658. Dr. Stephens died soon after the restoration.

The well-known *Bear Hotel* was for some years the early home of the distinguished portrait painter, Sir Thomas Lawrence, who had been born in Bristol, in 1769, and whose parents removed to this old hostelry in 1772. A lady who lived with the family has related how the child was accustomed to amuse himself by drawing pictures with a blacklead pencil. Of his first remarkable attempt at portrait drawing she gave a graphic account. " I perfectly recollect," she said, "as I was one afternoon sitting alone in the bar, watching him whip his top in the entrance hall, his running up to me and saying, ' Miss Lea, sit as you are and I will draw your picture.' I did as he desired, and in a few minutes he produced what was always considered an excellent likeness of me. He was at that time in petticoats, and I think not more than four years of age." The family left Devizes in 1779, and the young painter continued his career, securing fame, honours, and an income of between £10,000 and £20,000 per annum.

Devizes, or its immediate neighbourhood, was the birth-place of

JOSEPH RANDOLPH MULLINGS,

a gentleman who became widely and honourably known in North Wilts and East Gloucestershire. Mr. Mullings, who was born in 1792, came in early life to Cirencester, where by the skilful and diligent exercise of great natural abilities and high integrity of character, he secured an extensive legal practice, and established the firm now well known as that of Messrs.

Mullings, Ellett, and Co. While thus successful in his profession, he also gained the confidence and esteem of all classes. In 1848 he was returned as parliamentary representative for the borough, his election testifying to the personal respect in which he was held by his fellow townsmen, as well as to their sympathy with his political views. " He has," said one of his chief supporters, Mr. Charles Lawrence, when advocating his claims on a subsequent occasion, " no adventitious claims of birth, or rank, or fortune; he stands on his own personal merits. Let me invite the attention of the most humble men amongst you to the interesting and instructive fact that Mr. Mullings is indebted for his position to nothing but native talent, nursed and rendered productive by great industry and indomitable perseverance, which in this free country is open to the humblest born pursuing the same course." He proved in many important respects an excellent member of parliament, and was the author of some useful measures of legislation.

The diligent discharge of professional and public duties told upon his health, and in the spring of 1859 he resigned his seat and withdrew from active life. In the summer he accompanied some of his family to Montpellier in France, where he was seized with a violent pulmonary hemorrhage, and died after a brief illness, October 18, 1859. He was buried at Crudwell, in which parish, at Eastcourt House, he had resided for some years previous to his death.

Of a singular charity formerly dispensed in Devizes, and known as " The Coventry Dole," the following account has been given:—" A poor weaver passing through Devizes, without money and without friends, being overtaken by hunger and the utmost necessity, applied for charity to a baker, who, kindly gave him a penny loaf. The weaver made his way to Coventry, where after many years' industry, he amassed a fortune; and by his will, in remembrance of the seasonable charity of Devizes, he bequeathed a sum, in trust, for the purpose of distributing, on the anniversary of the day when he was so relieved, a halfpenny loaf to every person in the town, gentle and simple, and to every traveller that should pass through the town on that day a penny loaf. In the year 1786 the Archduke of Austria and his suite passed through the town on the day of the Coventry Loaf Dole,

I

on their way from Bath to London, when a loaf was presented to each of them, of which the Duke and Duchess were most cheerfully pleased to accept; and the custom struck the Archduke so forcibly, as a curious anecdote in his travels, that he minuted down the circumstance; and the high personages seemed to take delight in breakfasting on the loaf thus given, as the testimony of gratitude for a favour so seasonably conferred."

The Museum of the Wiltshire Archæological and Natural History Society is situated in Devizes. It was opened by Gabriel Goldney, Esq., M.P., the President of the Society, Sept. 8, 1784. It contains not only the Society's varied and interesting colllections, but also a valuable library of books.

Between here and the upper end of the county, many names will claim attention.

Two miles north-east of Devizes is the parish of *Rowde*, of which a Dr. Ferdinando Warner was vicar about 1730. He afterwards became rector of St. Michael's, Queenhithe, London, and was known as one of the most laborious authors of last century, writing numerous large volumes of theological and historical works. He is said to have written three folio volumes with one pen, a feat which throws into the shade the performance with which another old writer thus credits himself:—

> " With one sole pen I wrote this book,
>   Made of a gray goose quill;
> A pen it was when I it took,
> A pen I leave it still."

Among his works was *An Account of the Gout*, a disorder from which he long suffered, and of which he at length died at the age of 68.

Seven miles west, *Draycot*, in the parish of *Wilcot*, reminds us of an eminent Prelate,

DR. JOHN BUCKERIDGE,

one of Fuller's Wiltshire worthies, who was born here about 1562. In 1578 he became a student of St. John's College, Oxford, and after taking his degrees of arts, entered into holy orders. He soon obtained livings, and also became Chaplain to Archbishop Whitgift. From King James he not only received a presentation to the vicarage of St. Giles's, Cripplegate, London, but an appointment as one of His Majesty's Chaplains and installation as a canon of Windsor. He was a favourite with the King, before whom he preached on one occasion for the express purpose of turning some of the hard-headed Presbyterians from the error of their ways. Preferment still awaited him, and in 1611 he was raised to the see of Rochester, and in 1618 was translated to the richer bishopric of Ely. This new dignity he did not long hold, dying in 1621. His principal work is a controversial one against the Jesuit Bellarmin.

ROBERT NICHOLAS,

belonging to an ancient and honourable family, was born at *All Cannings* in 1597. He was educated for the law, and in 1640 being elected for Devizes, he served in the Long Parliament. He took an active part in the impeachment of Archbishop Laud. In 1648 he was appointed one of the assistant Judges in the trial of the King; but there is no proof that he took any part in the proceedings. The following year he was made a Judge of the Upper Bench, and a few years afterwards Oliver Cromwell made him Baron of the Exchequer. He appears to have retired into private life after the Restoration. A story setting his character in a favourable light, is told of his recognising in a royalist prisoner whom he was trying at Exeter, an old schoolfellow who had once generously borne a severe punishment for him at Westminster School. Although obliged to pass sentence of death upon him, he hurried to London and obtained from the Protector a pardon for the friend of his boyhood. The royalist, whose life was thus preserved, was William Wake, the father of the William Wake who became Archbishop of Canterbury in 1715.

The church of All Cannings contains several beautiful windows of stained glass, each presented by a different donor. The inscription under one is especially worthy of note :

" This window is dedicated to the honour and glory of Almighty God by Thomas Sotheron Estcourt, in memory of a friendship of more than 50 years between the houses of Methuen and Estcourt. We took sweet counsel together, and walked to the House of God as friends.—Ps. 55, 14."

The vicar of Bishops Cannings, of whom Aubrey gives us a graphic sketch, appears to have been of anything but a puritanical cast of mind.

"MR. FERRABY,

the minister of Bishops Cannings," the old writer says, "was an ingenious man, and an excellent musician, and made severall of his parishioners good musicians, both for vocall and instrumentall musick; they sung the Psalmes in consort to the organ, which Mr. Ferraby procured to be erected.

"When King James the First was in these parts he lay at Sir Edward Baynton's at Bromham. Mr. Ferraby then entertained his Majesty at the Bush, in Cotefield, with bucoliques of his own making and composing, of four parts; which were sung by his parishioners, who wore frocks and whippes like carters. Whilst his Majesty was thus diverted, the eight bells (of which he was the cause) did ring, and the organ was played on for state; and after this musical entertainment he entertained his Majesty with a foot-ball match of his own parishioners. This parish in those days would have challenged all England for musique, foot-ball, and ringing. For this entertainment his Majesty made him one of his chaplains in ordinary.

"When Queen Anne [Anne of Denmark, Queen of James I.] returned from Bathe, he made an entertainment for her Majesty on Canning's-down, sc. at Shepherds-shard, at Wensditch, with a pastorall performed by himself and his parishioners in shepherds' weeds. A copie of his song was printed within a compartment excellently well engraved and designed, with goates, pipes, sheep hooks, cornucopias, &c." His song, which Britton says Aubrey has given in his manuscript, was "voyc't in four parts compleatly musical;" and "was by her Highnesse not only most gratiously accepted and approved, but also bounteously rewarded; and by the right honourable, worshipfull, and the rest of the generall hearers and beholders, worthily applauded." The date of this entertainment was 11th June, 1613.

THOMAS STEVENS,

who in March, 1622, left *Bishops Cannings* a poor rustic boy, the son of a labouring man, became an apprentice in Bristol, of which city he was elected Mayor in 1668. He died in April, 1679, leaving lands to build and endow two large alms houses for 12 poor men and women in each; one in the parish of St. Philip and Jacob, and the other in the parish of the Temple. He also left among other bequests one of £10 to the poor of his native village.

Bishops Cannings was also the birthplace of

DR. JAMES POUND,

who was born in February, 1669. He belonged to an ancient and respectable family, and having entered the Church became rector of Wanstead, in Essex. A man of ability, genius, and enterprise, he distinguished himself as a divine, a physician, and mathematician. He went to the East Indies in the service of the Company, and narrowly escaped from the massacre of the factory at Pulo Condore, in 1705. His papers and a valuable collection of curiosities were all destroyed. He died at Wanstead, Nov. 16, 1724. Dr. Pound was the maternal uncle of an eminent Gloucestershire man, Dr. William Bradley, the astronomer royal, and afforded him those early instructions which led to his future successful career as a man of science.

The church organ, which in 1809 was erected at a cost of £400, was the gift of a native of the parish—

WILLIAM BAYLEY,

who also gave £600 to be invested for the payment of an organist, and the repairing of the instrument. Mr. Bayley was the son of a small farmer, but impelled by a strong desire for travel, he left the plough and went to sea. Having acquired some knowledge of navigation, he accompanied Captain Cook in his second voyage round the globe. Mr. Wales, the astronomer of the expedition, discovering his aptitude for astronomical pursuits, employed him as assistant in taking observations and making calculations. After his return he became head of the Royal Naval School, at Portsea. Having obtained considerable wealth, he resigned his post, and visiting his native village conferred upon it the benefit we have mentioned. He died in Dec., 1810.

The road running north-east from Devizes passes through a district of which it has been said there is none in the British Isles of greater interest to the antiquary. Here the way across the downs passes the Wansdyke and Shepherds Shord, and reaches Avebury and Silbury Hill, a locality rich in vast and mysterious ancient remains. Eastward, almost parallel with the Kennet, the road pursues its way to Marlborough, leaving on the south *West Overton*, a village that reminds us of George Farr, the stalwart carter, who with his own little boy, and an under carter, all perished on the downs, some of the many Wiltshire victims of the terrible snow storm of January 18th, 1881. Roundway Hill, in the parish of Bishops Cannings, and standing between that village and Bromham, was the scene of a fight in the civil war in 1643. The royalists under the Marquis of Hertford and Prince Maurice, having lost the battle of Lansdowne, retreated to Devizes. Sir William Waller followed in pursuit and invested the town; but on the approach of Lord Wilmot with 1500 men the Parliamentarians withdrew to Roundway. Here they occupied a strong position, but imprudently descending to attack their opponents suffered defeat.

DR. GEORGE WEBBE,

a prelate of eminence in the seventeenth century, was a native of *Bromham*. Nothing is known of the date of his birth or the incidents of his early life. He was rector of St. Peter and Paul, in Bath, and was appointed one of the chaplains of Charles I. In 1634 he was made Bishop of Limerick, in Ireland, but was thrown into prison by the Irish rebels in 1641, and there died of gaol fever. He was esteemed one of the best preachers of the time, and was the author of various books.

The Rev. John Collinson, author of *Beauties of British Antiquity*, and *The History and Antiquities of Somersetshire*, was rector of Bromham, when he published the former work in 1799.

The familiar name of Erin's great poet,

TOM MOORE,

is almost as much associated with Wiltshire as with his native land. The Marquis of Lansdowne, who had been his generous and steady friend through those periods of his life when he was writing his chief works and winning his great fame, found him a quiet and beautiful home in the neighbourhood of his own residence. Sloperton Cottage is but a short walk from Bowood. Here the genial-hearted poet passed nearly the last half of his life. Here, too, his life closed, and he found a grave, surrounded by scenes and friends he loved, in the peaceful churchyard of Bromham. A flat stone, enclosed by iron railings, records the decease of himself, his wife, and all their children. Many will read the inscription with tender interest :—

" Anastasia Mary Moore, born March 13, 1813, died March 8th, 1829.

" Also her brother, John Russell Moore, who died November 23rd, 1842, aged 19 years.

" And their father, THOMAS MOORE, tenderly beloved by all who knew the goodness of his heart; the Poet and Patriot of his country, Ireland. Born May 28, 1779 ; sank to rest Feb. 25th, 1852, aged 72. ' God is love.'

" Also his wife, Bessy Moore, who died 4th September, 1865.

" And to the memory of their dear son, Thomas Lansdowne Parr Moore, born 24th Oct., 1818; died in Africa, January, 1846."

This was for more than twenty-seven years the only memorial that marked the sleeping place of the gifted bard. A beautiful stained-glass window was some years ago inserted in the end of the church to the memory of his widow, and in 1879 a movement, led by his old friends Mr. and Mrs. S. C. Hall, resulted in the insertion of one at the west end to the memory of the poet himself. The subject is the Last Judgment, and on the lower margin of the lights is the following inscription :—

"This Window was placed in this Church by the combined Subscriptions of 200 Persons, who honour the memory of the Poet of all circles and the Idol of his own, THOMAS MOORE."

Bowood, the seat of the Marquis of Lansdowne, is a noble mansion in the Italian style, and was built by the Earl of Shelburne, in the middle of last century, considerable additions having been since made.

The name of

HENRY, 3RD MARQUIS OF LANSDOWNE,

must often occur in any such work as the present. His rank and character alike served to render him a prominent figure in Wiltshire records. This distinguished nobleman, who was the son of Earl Shelburne, was born July 2, 1780 : his father being raised to the Marquisate four years later. After spending some time at Westminster he was sent to Edinburgh, where he formed acquaintance with Brougham, Jeffery, Sidney Smith, and others who, like himself, became eminent public characters. He graduated at Cambridge, and after a tour on the Continent took his seat in the House of Commons as Lord Henry Petty, member for Calne. As one of the " All Talents Ministry" he was appointed Chancellor of the Exchequer, and at the same time was elected member for the University of Cambridge. His career, whether in or out of office, in the Commons or the Lords, was marked by the maintenance of the most liberal and humane principles. He nobly advocated the cause of the slave, persistently struggled for the abolition of the obnoxious laws against Nonconformists and Roman Catholics, and ever employed his eloquence on the side of philanthropy and freedom.

Succeeding his brother as Marquis in 1809, he greatly enlarged and beautified Bowood House. Here he delighted in the society of literary men and artists, whom he hospitably entertained, and to whom, in many instances, he proved a generous friend.

After serving in various Governments with great activity and ability, Lord Lansdowne declined an offer of the Premiership and took leave of the House of Lords in 1852. His influence, however, was still exercised, and on the death of the Duke of Wellington he was recognised as the most distinguished peer of the realm. The Queen sought his counsel, and he was induced to accept office in the Governments of Lord Aberdeen and Lord Palmerston. His active life closed January 31, 1863, at the age of 82.

A mile or so east of Bowood is the ancient borough of *Calne*. It is memorable as the scene of a great controversy on the question of celibacy, A.D. 977. A large number of ecclesiastics as well as many nobles assembled for conference and discussion. Dunstan was president. In the midst of the proceedings the floor of the large chamber in which they had met suddenly gave way. It was a fearful scene, many were killed, many more were injured. Dunstan, to whose wicked contrivance the event has been attributed, escaped unhurt. His escape was pronounced miraculous, and the miracle was interpreted as a Divine testimony in favour of celibacy, which was accordingly established!

From 1772 to 1779 Dr. Priestley and his family were resident in Calne. During this period he was literary companion to Lord Shelburne, who was then living at Bowood, and he here pursued his philosophical studies, and also wrote some of his educational and religious works. For some time, too, in the early part of the present century, the poet Bryan Walter Procter, better known as "Barry Cornwall," was here studying law and writing verses in a solicitor's office.

The gigantic white horse, in trotting attitude, which shows so conspicuously upon the side of Oldborough Castle Hill, near *Cherhill*, is said to be of remote origin. It was, however, greatly improved in form by the ingenuity and at the cost of Mr. Christopher Alsop, a surgeon residing at Calne, in the last century, who was described as a gentleman "not more remarkable for his professional skill than for his great mechanical genius and his integrity of character."

The name of yet another distinguished poet has to be here added to our list. Wiltshire has been singularly favoured as the resort and residence of sweet singers. With the names of Herbert, Crabbe, and Moore, as residents in the county, we associate that of the Rev.

WILLIAM LISLE BOWLES,

for forty-five years rector of *Bremhill*. Mr. Bowles was born Sept. 24, 1762, at King's Sutton, Northamptonshire, of which parish his father was vicar. He went to Winchester School, and afterwards entered Trinity. College, Oxford. Having taken holy orders, he was for some time at Uphill, near Weston-super-Mare. In 1803 he was made a prebendary of Salisbury, and in 1805 became rector of Bremhill. Here in the old gabled parsonage he lived a life congenial to his tastes. In his clerical duties and in literary pursuits he found varied and agreeable employment. He enjoyed the friendship of his neighbours, and took a lively interest in matters pertaining to the history and archæology of the county.

Mr. Bowles appeared in print as early as 1789, when he published *Fourteen Sonnets, written chiefly on Picturesque Spots during a journey*. These compositions breathed a fresh and natural spirit, very different to the laboured and artificial style of the period, and were received with great favour. Coleridge was one of the young poet's most ardent admirers, and Wordsworth and Southey also powerfully felt his influence. A new school of English poetry was thus formed, and the Lake poets, lovingly communing with nature, arose to sing their sweetly simple songs. Numerous other productions from the pen of Mr. Bowles followed, among the chief being *The Spirit of Discovery* and *The Missionary*. These works exhibit a fine appreciation of the beauties of nature, and abound in pure and generous sentiments. A controversy on some questions of criticism in the realm of poetry, in which Mr. Bowles was opposed by Byron and Campbell, excited much attention at the time. It was conducted with keen ability on both sides, but the victory was generally ascribed to the rector of Bremhill. His chief prose work was a *Life of Bishop Ken*, in two volumes.

Mr. Bowles lived to an advanced age, dying at Salisbury, 7th April, 1850, in his 88th year.

Of the amiable poet's eccentricity and absence of mind many tales are told. No one, however, but a bachelor would believe that he forgot the happy fact of his own marriage a few hours after its celebration! It requires, too, a considerable stretch of credulity to accept the tale of his having gone to a turnpike keeper's door to pay the toll, with a bridle in his hand but without a horse! It is more easy to believe that at one time he lived in such fear of mad dogs as to wear stout overalls to prevent being bitten; or, that he had the distance between his prebendal house and the cathedral measured to discover whether it would be in danger if the spire were to fall. Happier thoughts were associated with the glorious spire when he wrote :—

> When summer comes, the little children play
> In the churchyard of our cathedral gray,
> Busy as morning bees, and gathering flowers,
> In the brief sunshine; they, of coming hours
> Reck not, intent upon their play, though time
> Speed like a spectre by them, and their prime
> Bear on to sorrow—" Angel, cry aloud!
> Tell them of life's long evening—of the shroud."

No! let them play; for age alone, and care,
Too soon will frown to teach them what they are.
Then let them play; but come, with aspect bland,
Come, charity, and lead them by the hand;
Come, faith, and point amidst life's saddest gloom,
A light from Heaven, that shines beyond the tomb.
When they look up, and in the clouds admire
The lessening shaft of that aërial spire,
So be their thoughts uplifted from the sod,
Where time's brief flowers they gather—to their God.

A pretty legend, shedding an amiable light on the character of a former clergyman of *Winterbourne Monkton*, and investing its little churchyard with a sweet interest, is told by Canon Jackson. " The Rev.

JOHN BRINSDEN,

Vicar, who died 1719, was buried at the east end of the churchyard, and a Sarsen stone from his own glebe, was placed over his grave. The numerous snowdrops to be seen there in spring were originally planted by him in the form of letters of the alphabet, for the purpose, as it is said, of enlivening the dullness of the Horn-book to the young children of his parish school."

Kennett's *Parochial Antiquities* affords a glimpse of an ancient hayward of *Winterbourne Bassett*. " Old Simon Bransdon, of Winterbourne Bassett, in Wilts, had been parish clerk in the reign of Queen Mary, and was afterwards hayward of the town ; he was wont in the summer time to leave his oxen in the field and go to church and pray to St. Catherine, the tutelar saint of the church ; and when he returned, if any of his herd were stung with the gadfly and ran away, he would run after them and cry out, ' Pray, good St. Catherine of Winterbourne, stay my oxen ; pray, good St. Catherine, stay my oxen."

While Robert Raikes is justly honoured as the Founder of the Sunday School system, many others are rightly credited with earlier efforts of a similar kind. Among these

THOMAS BENET

is a notable and interesting instance. During the Sunday School Centenary celebration in the summer of 1880, the Rev. John A. Lloyd, vicar of Broad Hinton, gave publicity to the following facts :—

Thomas Benet, Esq., of Salthrop House, Wilts, by Deed 2nd June, 1743, endowed a day school in the parishes of Broad Hinton and Wroughton with the sum of £20 yearly to each school, and a house and land for the master's use, "that such children should be taught and instructed, between the ages of six and 15 years, to read perfectly their mother tongue, to write a good plain and fair handwriting in the Roman character, and to cast accounts, and should be educated and instructed in the Catechism and true principles and doctrines of the Church of England, and should constantly attend divine service in the parish church to which they respectively belong,"

At the same date rules and regulations were made for the Sunday School. "They (the children) shall be brought to Church as often as Divine Service shall be performed, and directed to behave themselves there with all Reverence, according to the Rubric, and join in making the responses. They shall come to the School on every Lord's Day at ten o'clock in the morning and two in the afternoon, and on Holy days at ten in the morning and attend the master to Church, who shall note the absent, and correct them at their next coming to school, not having a reasonable excuse." Prayers are directed to be taught the children, and Grace before and after meat. Public catechising is also enjoined. It thus appears that 37 years before Raikes commenced his successful movement at Gloucester, the plan of Sunday instruction for the children of the poor was being carried into effect in the rural parishes of Broad Hinton and Wroughton.

An interesting connection between the Right Hon. John Bright and Wiltshire was traced some few years ago by Mr. William Robertson, in his book on the Life and Times of the Quaker Statesman. He states that "The line of ancestry of the Bright family can be traced back to a respectable farmer named Abraham Bright and Martha, his wife, who resided at a farm near the pretty village of *Lyneham* (not far from Bradenstoke Priory), a pleasant dairy country in Wiltshire. At the present time the farm, which is situate in the parish of Christian Malford, bears the name of 'Bright's Farm,' and belongs to Sir Henry Meux, Bart. In the year 1714, Abraham Bright married a pretty Jewess named Martha Jacobs, and resided at Lyneham many years in a cottage (near the Parsonage), which was surrounded by an orchard of an acre and a quarter in area, but the cottage fell into ruins in the latter part of the last century, and the last group of apple trees died about fifty years ago, yet the name survives, for the spot is still called 'Bright's Orchard.' The handsome Jewess and her husband removed to Coventry and had several children, among whom was William Bright, who married twice. By his first wife, Mary Goode, were several children, one of whom was Jacob Bright. He married Martha Lucas, who had eight children, the youngest of whom was Jacob Bright. He came to Rochdale in 1796, and was the father of John Bright.

A recent writer in the *Wilts and Gloucestershire Standard* adds :—" The room or chapel in which they worshipped now forms part of a dwelling-house at Lyneham Green, on the Calne road. The Quaker's burying ground was at Goatacre. A Primitive Methodist chapel has recently been erected on the spot. There is an excellent pitched stone causeway leading to it from the hamlet, and it is surrounded by a well-built stone wall."

We will let Aubrey tell of

SIR HENRY DANVERS,

of whom, writing under the head of " Soldiers," he says: " Sir Henry Danvers, Knight, Earl of Danby and Baron of Dauntsey, was born at Dauntsey, 28th day of June, Ano Dni. 1573. He was of a magnificent and munificall spirit, and made that noble physic-garden at Oxford, and endowed it with, I thinke, 30 li per annum. In the epistles of Degory Wheare, History Professor of Oxford, in Latin, are several addressed to his Lordship that doe recite his worth. He allowed three thousand pounds per annum only for his kitchin. He bred up several brave young gentlemen and preferred them ; *e.g.*, Colonel Legg, and severall others, of which enquire further of my Lady Viscountesse Purbec. The estate of Henry Earle of Danby was above eleven thousand pounds per annum—near twelve. He died January 20th, 1643, and lies buried in a little chapell made for his monument on the north side of Dauntsey church, near to the spot where his father and ancestors lye." He died, the monument says, "full of honour, wounds, and days ;" but neither that nor Aubrey's pen refers to the part he took in the murder of Henry Long.

The prevalence at one time of high Calvinist opinions in the north of Wilts was largely due to the teaching and influence of the puritan

DR. TOBIAS CRISP,

who was for some years rector of *Brinkworth*. The son of a rich father, who filled high civic offices in the metropolis, Tobias was born in Bread-street, London, in 1600, and successively educated at Eton, Cambridge, and Oxford. On leaving the latter university, he became rector of Brink-worth, in 1627. Here, Dr. Gill says, " he was much followed for his edifying way of preaching, and for his hospitality to all persons that resorted to his house. As he had a plentiful estate of his own, he was liberal and hospitable to strangers that came far and near to attend upon his ministry ; and, according to good information from some of his descendants, a hundred persons, yea, and many more, have been entertained in his house at one and the same time, and ample provision made for man and beast." Apart from guests, his table would seem to have been at all times well surrounded, as his own family contained thirteen children. The account, too, awakens the suspicion that some of the preacher's followers, like a certain multitude of old, were influenced by " the loaves and fishes" so freely dispensed.

On the breaking out of the civil war, Dr. Crisp suffered from the insolence of the Cavalier soldiers, and retired to London. Here his religious opinions quickly brought him into much controversy with some of the city divines ; and Anthony Wood tells us " he was baited by fifty-two opponents in a grand dispute," concerning some of the doctrines he so dogmatically taught. In the midst of this polemical strife, in which he eagerly engaged, he took small-pox, and died Feb. 27, 1642. Many editions of his works have been published, under the title of *Christ alone exalted*, his writings being held in high esteem by those who entertained similar religious sentiments. Among his discourses is one occasioned by the death of a neighbouring minister—a Mr. Brunsell, vicar of Wroughton, who appears to have held the same doctrines as Crisp, whom he selected to preach his funeral sermon from the text, " Though we or an angel from heaven preach any other gospel unto you than that which we have preached unto you, let him be accursed," Gal. i. 8 : words which poor erring mortals have too often rashly adopted and applied.

However low the estimate which Henry VIII. set upon the lives of others, he appears to have held his own royal existence in high value, if we may judge by the liberal benefactions he bestowed upon those who on some occasions were the means of preserving it. Garsdon was the reward of Moody for saving the corpulent King from an ignominious death in a ditch, and the gift of Grittenham manor, in Brinkworth parish, was the expression of his gratitude to a surgeon whose skill cured him of a dangerous disorder. "King Henry 8," says Aubrey, "was dangerously ill of a Fistula, which—Ayliff, a famous Chirurgian at London cured : for which he had this great Estate given, and I thinke all the rest of his Estate hereabout."

Wootton Bassett, which some writers have erroneously described as the birthplace of Richard III., is an ancient borough, situated on high ground, affording fine views of this fertile and well-cultivated part of the county. It possesses the remains of a ducking stool, an instrument which our ancestors, in "the good old times," barbarously employed for the punishment of scolding women.

Old Swindon, a small market town, standing on a fine hill, has grown into importance during the railway age, while *New Swindon*, a creation of the same period, occupying a site which was formerly a marsh, is a still more considerable town, and one of the largest railway junctions in the kingdom.

Pleasantly situated and historically interesting, the village of *Purton* cannot be passed without notice. Here the Hyde family long held property and occasionally resided. The house now known as College Farm, at Purton Stoke, was at one time occupied by the famous Earl Clarendon, and here his daughter Anne Hyde, who became wife of the Duke of York, afterwards James II., and mother of Queen Mary, wife of William III., and Queen Anne, was born. The noble parish church of St. Mary, with its two towers, contains a monument to the celebrated

DR. NEVIL MASKELYNE,

the astronomer royal, who was a member of the Wiltshire Maskelyne family, and was buried here in 1811. The name of Dr. Maskelyne, who was born in 1732, was widely known both in Britain and through Europe as one of the most eminent astronomers of his time. He was the author of *The Mariner's Guide*, and his name is associated with several important observations and discoveries.

The hamlet of Bradon, in this parish, was a forest until 1665. One of its traditions, dating from the time of King John, is a romantic story of a Shropshire baron, Fulke Fitzwarine, who was in rebellion against that mean monarch. Fitzwarine, in the course of his movements, came with his followers to Bradon Forest, where for a time they lay concealed. " One day," we are told, "there came ten merchants, who brought from foreign lands rich clothes, and other valuable merchandise, which they had bought for the King and Queen of England, with money furnished from the royal treasury. As the convoy passed under the wood, followed by 24 sergeants-at-arms to guard the King's goods, John Fitzwarine was sent out to inquire who they were. John met with a rude reception; but Fulke and his companions came forwards, and in spite of their obstinate resistance, captured the whole party, and carried them with their convoy into the forest. When Fulke heard that they were the King's merchants, and that the loss would not fall upon their own heads, he ordered the rich clothes and furs to be brought forth, and measuring them out with his lance, gave to all his men their shares, each according to his degree and deserts. He then sent the merchants to the King, bearers of his grateful thanks for the fine robes with which his Majesty had clad all his good men."

Of the parish of *Minety*, the chief part of which was formerly included in Gloucestershire, but is now wholly in Wilts, Aubrey gives some curious scraps of information. " In Minety Common, in Bredon forest," he says, " neer the rode which leadeth to Ashton Caynes, is a boggy place called the Gogges, where is a spring, or springs, rising up out of fuller's earth. This puddle in hot and dry weather is candid like a hoar frost : which to the tast seems nitrous. . . . After a shower this spring will smoake." " The fuller's earth at Minety-common, when I tooke it up, was as black as black polished marble ; but having carried it in my pocket five or six days, it became gray." "At Mintie is an abundance of wild mint, from whence the village is denominated."

With Minety, as with Lyneham, a great Quaker name is associated. The ancestors of William Penn were at one time residents in this parish. Aubrey says "Sir William Penn, Vice Admiral, was born at Minety. His father was a keeper in Bradon forest : the lodge is called Penn's lodge to this day. He was father to William Penn, Esq., Lord Proprietor of Pensylvania ; it is a very ancient family in Buckinghamshire." Aubrey is wrong in making Sir William a Wiltshire man. The facts are these :—

Some four centuries or so ago a branch of the Penn family came from Buckinghamshire and settled here. One of these—a William Penn—died at an advanced age March 12th, 1591, and is buried in Minety Church. His son William, who died before him, left two sons, both of whom, after their grandfather's death, removed to Bristol. One of them, Giles, entered the Royal Navy, and distinguished himself as an enterprising seaman and a brave commander. He was the father of a son who was born in Bristol, 1621, and received the name of William. Following his father's profession, he was made a captain at twenty-one, and attained the rank of Sea General at thirty-two. Having served Cromwell, he continued to fill his post after the restoration, and was commander under the Duke of York in the great sea fight with the Dutch in 1665. For this service he was knighted. He lies buried in Redcliffe Church, Bristol, where there is a monument to his memory. This old sea lion was the father of William Penn, the Quaker; the Apostle of Peace and the Founder of Pennsylvania.

We may remark that Thomas Clarkson dedicated his *Life of Penn*, published in 1813, to a Wiltshire man, Henry Richard, Lord Holland, as " a vindicator of the rights of injured Africa, a friend to peace and constitutional reform, and a patron of civil and religious liberty."

Mrs. Marshall, in *Memoirs of Troublous Times*, tells a sad tale, gathered from family records, of two sons of Oliffe Richmond, of *Ashton Keynes*. On the commencement of the civil war, one followed the standard of the King and the other joined the Parliamentarian forces. These differences of opinion and action did not destroy brotherly affection, and on the night

K

preceding the battle of Newbury, one of them went in the dark into the camp of the other army. Eluding the vigilance of the sentinels he reached his brother's tent in the hope of an affectionate interview previous to the uncertain events of the morrow. On entering the tent, his brother, alarmed at the sudden appearance of a stranger, as he conceived him to be, rose upon his bed and shot him dead upon the spot !

The ancestors of the excellent Legh Richmond, author of the *Dairyman's Daughter* and other works, were at one time resident in the old Manor House, in this village.

Fuller tells us of one

ROBERT CANUTUS,

who, he says, " though his name might lead us to think he was a Dane," was born in the ancient borough of *Cricklade*. " Our Canutus," says the old writer, " went hence to Oxford, and there became chief of the canons of St. Fridsworth. He gathered the best flowers out of Pliny's ' Natural History,' and composing it into ' A Garland' (as he calleth it), dedicated the book to King Henry the Second. He also wrote his ' Comments' on the greater part of the Old and New Testament, and flourished anno 1170."

Branches of the Akerman family have for many generations past resided in various parts of Wilts. The name is most commonly found in the north division, particularly in and around Cricklade. From one of these branches, formerly residing at *Eisey*,

JOHN YONGE AKERMAN

was descended. Dr. Thirlwall, late Bishop of St. David's, in an address before the Royal Society of Literature, in 1874, says Mr. Akerman " was born in London, June 12, 1806 : his father having been for some years engaged in mercantile pursuits in that city, to which he had removed, [at the age of fifteen] from [Eisey] Wiltshire, where his family had previously resided for centuries." The Bishop proceeds to give some interesting particulars of Mr. Akerman's career, and we learn that " in early life he was private secretary to the famous William Cobbett, and subsequently for many years Secretary to the Directors of the London and Greenwich

Railway, which was fully opened Dec. 26, 1838. During a part, too, of this time he was private secretary to Lord Albert Conyngham (afterwards Lord Londesborough), a post to which he was naturally recommended by the kindred tastes existing between them in the study of antiquities, especially those of England, to which from his early youth he had been exceedingly attached."

Mr. Akerman, who in 1834 had been elected a member of the Society of Antiquaries, became joint secretary with Sir Henry Ellis, K.H., of the Society in 1848. Five years later he became its sole Secretary. The failure of his health obliged him in 1860 to resign this office, and leaving London he retired to reside at Abingdon, where he acted as local Secretary of the Society for Berkshire, and in other ways continued to do good service to Archæology till within a short period of his death. This event occurred at Abingdon, after a brief illness, May 18, 1873.

An obituary notice in the Wiltshire Magazine, Vol. XIV., referred to his numerous publications, and described him as well known in his official character as Secretary to the Society of Antiquaries, and as a literary man by his works on archæological subjects.

The learned prelate, from whom we have already quoted, gives a list of the separate publications which he knew to have proceeded from his active pen. It contains no fewer than 22 works on various archæological subjects, particularly Numismatics, to which he devoted great attention and on which he has become an acknowledged authority. *A Glossary of Wiltshire Provincial Words and Phrases*, and *Wiltshire Tales in Prose and Verse*, are included in the number. In addition to these his detached papers in *The Numismatic Journal*, which he originated : *The Numismatic Chronicle*, which he edited ; the *Archæologia ;* the *Proceedings of the Society of Antiquaries* ; and elsewhere, numbered 126. These varied and valuable labours were highly appreciated and variously acknowledged. The Gold Medal of the French Institute was conferred upon him, and he was elected an honorary member of several Foreign as well as British Societies.

Of his devotion to his chosen pursuits and his unselfish and self-sacrificing character, Dr. Thirlwall bore the following testimony :—

" At the Society of Antiquaries, besides his special duties as Secretary, he devoted much time to the general encouragement of those who were willing to devote their time or their money to archæological researches, setting them the good example of conducting in person during his days of vacation, for five or six years, some of the most successful excavations which have been carried out during recent years. Indeed, there can be little doubt that exposure for many successive days to cold and wet autumnal weather on the bare and exposed downs of Wiltshire was the immediate cause of the acute rheumatism, which, in the end, broke down utterly a frame of great natural strength. and crippled bodily energies, which, with a little more care, might have been efficient even now. It was, in fact, the habit of our deceased friend to think of others, and to forget himself ; thus, after a long and fatiguing day's labour, he was always to be found at work, often till a late hour of the evening, denying to himself only the repose necessary to keep the mind in a true state of health."

In the baptismal register of the parish of *Hannington* may be found the name of

DR. NARCISSUS MARSH,

who rose to be Archbishop of Armagh and Primate of Ireland. He was the son of William and Grace Marsh, who had come out of Kent and purchased a small property in this village. Here he was born in 1638. At the age of sixteen he entered Magdalen Hall, Oxford, and was elected fellow of Exeter College four years afterwards. He was vicar of Swindon for one year, 1662. Having taken his D.D. degree in 1671, he was made principal of St. Alban's Hall, 1673. Under the patronage of the Duke of Ormond he obtained preferment after preferment till, in 1703, he reached the Archbishopric of Armagh. Dr. Marsh was learned and charitable, the author of several works, the builder of a noble Library in Dublin, which he enriched with valuable books ; and the founder of almshouses for clergymen's widows at Drogheda. He died in 1713, aged 75.

PART V.

—◆—

EAST WILTS.—*NORTH*.

 ROSSING one of our imaginary division lines we leave the North
end of Mid Wilts, and entering that of East Wilts, turn
Southward and take our way down the East side of the county.
A tomb in the Parish Church of Bourton-on-the-Hill, in
Gloucestershire, bears the following simple inscription :—

"Underdeath this tomb lies buried
the Body of
SAMUEL WILSON WARNEFORD, LL.D.,
Forty-four years Rector of this Parish,
Who died the 11th of January, MDCCCLV.,
Aged 92 years.
To do good and to distribute forget not, for with such
sacrifices God is well pleased."

THE long life, the close of which is thus briefly recorded, was one of such
singular Christian philanthropy, that it claims more than passing notice.
Dr. Warneford was born in 1763, at Warneford Place, in the hamlet of
Sevenhampton, near *Highworth*. He was the son of the Rev. Francis
Warneford, and grandson of Richard Warneford, D.D., vicar of St.
Martin's, York. This family is one of the most ancient in North Wilts,

and may be traced from the period of the first Crusade. Aubrey gives from "an old, and very faire and gilt and painted MS. in folio on velam," an extract from a deed in which one of the Warneford family "confirms to God and the Chapel of St. James of Sevenhampton, and to Elias there, a house and land which . . . Warn . . . my father, of good memory, gave to found a daily mass for his soul, with *Dirige* and *Placebo*, &c." Another extract which runs thus: "9 Aug. The obit. of John Warneford, A.D. 1393," probably supplies both the founder's name and the year. Another of the same name was sheriff of Wilts in 1589, and Sir Edmund in 1683. During the Civil Wars the Warnefords were Parliamentarians. The south-east chapel in Highworth church belongs to the family, many members of which are buried in the south aisle. A portion of the estates, descending in the male line from the time of King John, is still held by the Rev. John Henry Warneford, of Warneford Place.

In 1779 Samuel was entered as a commoner of University College, Oxford. At the age of twenty he graduated B.A., and in 1786 M.A. In 1790 he took the degree of B.C.L., and that of D.C.L. grand compounder in 1810. In 1796 he married Margaret, daughter of Edward Loveden Loveden, Esq., M.P., but became a widower a few years afterwards. His wife's fortune devolved upon him at her decease. His own income also much exceeded his expenditure. He had no children, and for the younger members of his family considerable provision had been made at the marriage of his parents. Under these circumstances Dr. Warneford resolved to devote his wealth to the glory of God and the welfare of his fellow men. As a country clergyman—first as rector of Lydiard Millicent, and afterwards rector of Bourton-on-the-Hill and Moreton-in-the-Marsh —his life was favourable to the contemplative habits of his benevolent mind. So large, thoughtful, and original were his methods and benefactions, that it has been well said, "There is to be found in Dr. Warneford's love of mankind, that variety, comprehensiveness, and intermixture of pious and charitable purposes which we shall look for in vain in any past dedications of thought and property for the benefit of man."

It would be impossible in our limited space to give anything like a full account of the varied and novel directions in which his munificence found glad exercise. A few, however, must be mentioned. That admirable institution, now known as the Warneford Lunatic Asylum, near Oxford, for "the charitable care and cure of the afflicted of the middle classes of society, labouring under poverty, but not reduced to pauperism, was the first great undertaking which engaged his favour, and at length rivetted his philanthropy to such merciful provisions." His endowment of the Warneford Prize in Queen's College, Birmingham, and his princely benefactions to that and its cognate Institution, the Queen's Hospital, again and again received the grateful acknowledgments of the governors, who have shown their sense of these benefits by placing his bust in marble on the staircase of the latter noble edifice. The establishment of the Leamington Bathing Institution and Hospital, large donations to King's College Hospital and similar institutions in London, liberal support to the Canterbury Clergy Orphan Institution, and numerous other charitable objects, were among his manifold deeds of love and mercy. To the erection of schools and the extension of Church accommodation he not only gave large sums of money, but devoted much time and effort. On one occasion he writes "I have been to Hawkesbury, on the Hillsley proposed Church; to Stroud, on the Whiteshill Church; to Monmouth, for correct information on Cinderford Church; to Gloucester, on the Twyford and Langford Chapel; and to Cheltenham, to forward the Leckhampton Church." He substantially repaired his own two parish churches at Bourton and Moreton, re-fitting and improving their interiors, at the cost of about £1000 each. Many other churches partook of his bounty, which was not confined to their erection, but in some cases extended to their permanent endowment. On another occasion he says "Applications from prelates of all climes, also for churches, parsonage-houses, schools, &c., foreign from my own diocese, overwhelm me." But to these appeals there was commonly some generous response, and his bounty flowed in free streams, not only to different parts of Britain, but to the most distant colonies. The total amount of these gifts it is impossible to tell, but we are assured, upon good grounds, that " he personally, by his own act and deed, settled upon works of surpassing usefulness" sums of money amounting to £200,000.

The spirit in which all this munificence was dispensed, while intensely earnest, was singularly free from ostentation. Constrained by the highest motives, he did his deeds, "as to the Lord, and not unto men." In their performance he found an amount of happiness such as no course of mere worldly self-indulgence could ever afford. Numerous extracts from his correspondence prove the elevation of his sentiments and the serenity of his mind. Many of these are worthy of being written in letters of gold. Here is a specimen of the spirit and manner in which he gave : "As life is uncertain, before I retire to rest this night I am anxious to fulfil my promise to you, and I send you a cheque on Hoare's for £500, and I am confident you cannot feel so much pleasure in receiving as I do in presenting it to you." He rejoiced in the benevolent activity of others :— "It is delightful to see fellow-labourers sedulously employed *in promoting the glory of God and the good of man!* What a *blessing* to be permitted to be *thus employed!*" His posthumous donations to religious and charitable objects were large and numerous. We cannot better close this brief sketch than with the words of his friend the Rev. Vaughan Thomas, from whose memoir of him we have gathered most of the foregoing particulars. "Finally, it may be said, upon a careful survey of all he did and gave, of all he designed and proposed under the various relations of his Christian philanthropy, that no wants of man were too great for his energies, nor too small for his thoughtful care and attention."

The late Lady Wetherell Warneford, the niece of Dr. Warneford, in fulfilment of the intentions of her uncle, bequeathed large funds for the foundation of the now well-known Warneford Ecclesiastical and Clerical Charities. For the former of these, £30,000 is vested in trustees to apply the net annual income in promoting the building, re-building, and repairing of Churches and Parsonages in Districts *principally inhabited by the Poor :* and for the latter £45,000, the annual income of which is to be used in aiding necessitous widows and orphans of the poorer and deserving clergy. The operation of these great charities is limited to that part of the Diocese of Gloucester and Bristol which comprised the ancient Diocese of Gloucester.

The ancient church of St. Andrew, in the parish of *Wanborough*, is remarkable as having a square Perpendicular tower at the west end, and also a spire between the chancel and the nave. This peculiarity, which also marks the parish church of Purton, is found nowhere else in England except at Ormskirk, Lancashire.

The pleasantly situated little town of *Ramsbury* claims some notice as having been the seat of Ethelstan and Odo, the first and second bishops of the diocese formed by Plegmund, Archbishop of Canterbury early in the tenth century. Of *Littlecote* in this parish, Camden writing nearly three centuries ago, says "it is remarkable for its Lord, John Popham, who exercised the office of Judge of the King's Court with the highest applause." It was also remarkable as the residence of the Darells, one of whom, living in the time of Queen Elizabeth, gained an infamous notoriety. "William Darell, Esq.," as he was sometimes styled, or "Wild Darell," as he is more commonly called, judged in the most favourable light appears to have been a reckless and unprincipled man. Tradition brands him as the murderer of a newly born illegitimate babe, of which he was the father; and relates how, though he escaped the gallows, he yet broke his neck over a stone stile. There is reason to doubt the strict accuracy of the legend, but had it no foundation? Scott gives it, greatly altered, in a ballad in *Rokeby*.

Leland, itinerating through Wiltshire, writes :—" From *Ramesbyri* on to *Marlebyri*, a three miles [read six] by hilly grounde, fruitful of corn and wood. About half a mile on I cam into Marlebyri, I passed over a broke that cam down north west from the hills, and so ran by south east into the streme of *Kenet*, about half-a-mile bynethe Marlebyri. The towne of Marlebyri standith in lengthe from the top of an hill flat east to a valley lyinge flat weste." He proceeds to speak of its chief features. For centuries before the old traveller's time Marlborough had been a place of note. In 1267 Henry III. held a parliament, or a general assembly of the "Estates of England," here. The special object for which it was convened was to provide for "the better state of the realm, and the more speedy administration of justice." The laws known as the "Statutes of Marlbridge" for the suppression of tumults were enacted at this time. Marlborough has continued from time to time to make some figure in history;

and is at present of, perhaps, greater interest and importance than at any period of its history. Several of its natives and residents have acquired more or less celebrity.

OBADIAH SEDGWICK,

who was born here, in 1600, and educated at Queen's College, Oxford, having embraced puritanical and republican principles took an active part in the times of the civil war and commonwealth. He frequently preached before the Parliament, and published several sermons and tracts. He died in his native town, in 1657. A William Sedgwick, probably of the same family, is said to have been a man of fanatical spirit, and was known as "Doom's day Sedgwick," for professing to foretell the day of Judgment.

DR. HENRY SACHAVERELL,

the son of a Marlborough clergyman, gained great notoriety and valuable preferment by the part he played as champion of the Church in Queen Anne's reign. The fanatical enthusiasm with which this zealot was then hailed would find but faint echoes now ; and few would regard him as reflecting any honour upon the place of his birth. The causes of his ephemeral popularity may, however, be briefly told. Having been appointed to preach before the Lord Mayor and Sheriffs of London he delivered an inflammatory discourse in which, censuring the Revolution, he raised the cry of 'the Church in danger ;' hotly denounced nonconformists, and expatiated on the imaginary evils of religious toleration. This harangue he published, dedicating it to the Lord Mayor ; and forty thousand copies were quickly sold. The government unwisely prosecuted the preacher, and his trial greatly excited the wrath of his party. He escaped with so lenient a sentence that his supporters celebrated it as a triumph, and Sachaverell was glorified as the hero of the hierarchy. On the expiration of his three years of suspension from preaching he was appointed to the valuable rectory of St. Andrew's, Holborn. At a subsequent period, under the influence of his name and sentiments, riots took place in Birmingham, Bristol, and other places, in which several dwelling houses and places of worship of dissenters were demolished. Despised by those who had made him their tool, and squabbling with his own parishioners, the unenviable popularity of Sachaverell had subsided long before his death in 1724.

The ancient mansion long known to travellers in coaching days as the "Castle Inn," and now familiar to young Marlburians as the "Old House," was formerly the residence of the Duchess of Somerset. She was the patron and friend of the poet Thomson, who here composed his poem on *Spring*, which he published in 1728, and which forms part of *The Seasons*.

Pope, Congreve, Addison, and other distinguished men of letters recognised the poetical merits of

JOHN HUGHES,

who was born at Marlborough, January 29, 1677. His grandfather, William Hughes, M.A., a native of Bromham, had been ejected for nonconformity from the vicarage of St. Mary's, in 1662. John, who was named after his father, and whose mother belonged to an ancient Wiltshire family named Burges, received his early education at private schools in London, where his parents went to reside; and subsequently went to a dissenting academy, of which the Rev. Thos. Rowe was tutor; and where he had Isaac Watts as a fellow student. The delicate state of his health unfitting him for active employment, his attention was early given to poetry, music, and drawing. He obtained a post in the Ordnance department, the duties of which being light allowed him much leisure for literary pursuits. His first poem on the peace of Ryswick, published when he was only twenty years of age, was well received, as was also his second, *The Court of Neptune*, which followed two years after. He became associated with Steele, Addison, and others, and wrote for the *Tatler*, *Spectator*, and *Guardian*. He also distinguished himself as a friend to religious toleration by a work which he wrote in reply to a sermon by Dr. Willis, Dean of Lincoln. His last work—a drama, entitled the *Siege of Damascus*, was presented on the stage the night of his death. Intelligence of its favourable reception was brought to his dying bed, but his mind fixed upon higher things was unmoved by the communication. He died 17th February, 1720.

His works were collected and published in two volumes by his brother-in-law, Mr. W. Duncombe, in 1735.

A younger brother,—

JABEZ HUGHES,

excelled as a scholar, translating several Latin and Spanish works. He also wrote various miscellaneous pieces in prose and verse. He died in 1731, aged 46.

SIR MICHAEL FOSTER,

a learned judge, who filled high offices during the middle of last century, was a native of Marlborough. He was elected recorder of Bristol in 1737, and in 1745 was made a justice of the King's Bench, and knighted. He published several works, and died in 1765, aged 74. His life was written by his nephew,—

MICHAEL DODSON,

also a native of Marlborough. Dodson, who was the son of a Dissenting minister, studied for the law, and was called to the bar in 1783. Much of his attention seems to have been directed to Biblical literature, and he published in 1790 a translation of Isaiah with notes. He died in 1799, aged 67.

WALTER HARTE,

another native of this town, was the writer of some poetical pieces which have been much admired, and also a history of Gustavus Adolphus in two vols. He died 1773.

Four or five miles south east of Marlborough is "Majestic Savernake"— an ancient and extensive forest surrounding the residence of its proprietor, the Marquis of Ailesbury. It is one of the most beautiful parts of the county, rich in scenery and traditions. *Savernake Forest* was formed into an ecclesiastical parish in 1864. The Church of St. Katharine, a handsome stone Gothic edifice, was erected at the cost of the Marchioness of Ailesbury in memory of her mother, the Countess of Pembroke. The schoolroom, and organist's and sacristan's houses were built by the Marquis of Ailesbury, who is sole landowner.

PART VI.

EAST WILTS.—*SOUTH*.

"It is of unspeakable advantage to possess our minds with an habitual good intention, and to aim all our thoughts, words, and actions at some laudable end, whether it be the glory of our Maker, the good of mankind, or the benefit of our own souls."

ADDISON.

"True humanity consists not in a squeamish ear; nor in starting and shrinking at tales of misery; but in a disposition of heart to relieve it."   C. J. FOX.

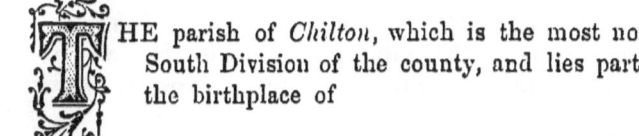HE parish of *Chilton*, which is the most northerly point in the South Division of the county, and lies partly in Berkshire, was the birthplace of

DR. ANTHONY SADLER,

who was chaplain to Charles II. He wrote tracts, sermons, and also a *Divine Masque* which he dedicated to General Monk. He died in 1680.

About three miles south of Chilton, and nearly the same distance west from Hungerford, is the village of *Froxfield*, notable for Somerset Hospital, a group of Almshouses founded in 1686, by Sarah Duchess Dowager of Somerset. By the munificence of this lady thirty widows of laymen and twenty widows of clergymen from parts of England within one hundred and fifty miles of London, are here provided with a home and an annual allowance of £36 each. The trustees of this great charity are chiefly chosen from the nobility and gentry of the county.

DR. THOMAS WILLIS,

one of the most eminent physicians and medical writers of the seventeenth century, was born at *Great Bedwin* in 1621. He was a student of Christchurch, Oxford, where he took his degrees in arts and medicine. He took up arms for Charles I. when Oxford was garrisoned, but after that city had surrendered he resumed his professional studies and practice, and married Mary, daughter of Dr. Fell, Dean of Christ Church. In 1660 he was appointed Sedleian Professor of natural philosophy. Removing to London in 1666 he soon rose to great professional distinction. His works were numerous and learned, and his moral character high. He died in 1675, and found a grave in Westminster Abbey.

A mile or so south from Savernake station is a little red brick house with tall chimneys. It is known as the Laundry, and is all that now remains of a mansion in which nobility once dwelt, and where a royal marriage was once celebrated. *Wulfhall*, in the parish of *East Grafton*, was long the residence of the Seymour family, several members of which figure conspicuously in English history. Sir John Seymour, who resided here in the first part of the sixteenth century, and died in 1536, was the father of a large family, of which a daughter and two sons rose to exalted positions.

Of the early life of the daughter,—

JANE SEYMOUR,

little is known except that she received part of her education in France. Becoming maid of honour to Anne Boleyn she attracted the notice of the King, and unhappily gained his affections. Occasion was soon found against the Queen, who was charged with unfaithfulness, and being sent to the Tower, was there beheaded. The spring day on which this tragedy was being enacted Henry was with his bride elect at Wulfhall, and the very day after this execution of his second wife he took Jane Seymour as his third. The marriage festivities were held in a fine old barn. This building, made of wood and thatched, is still standing. It is 57 yards long and nearly nine wide. It is said that some of the nails and hooks to which the decorations were attached are still to be seen. The coronation of Queen Jane, which was delayed on account of a pestilence, never took place, and her life of royalty was of short duration. In 1537, about eighteen months after her marriage, she gave birth to a son, Edward VI., and died thirteen days afterwards. She was buried at Windsor.

Wulfhall was subsequently visited by the King, who on Saturday, Aug. 9, 1539, came with his whole court and spent the three following days with

EDWARD SEYMOUR,

the late young Queen's brother, who had been raised to the peerage as Earl of Hertford. To this brother-in-law Henry appears to have been partial, for he was at Wulfhall again in August, 1543. In less than three years and a half from this date the life of the King had closed; and his young son, not yet ten years old, succeeded him, as Edward VI. Henry had willed a regency during the minority of the young King, and of the sixteen executors who were appointed, Earl Hertford was elected President. He was also made guardian of his royal nephew, and receiving the title of Duke of Somerset, he held the high office of Protector of England, and exercised government over the whole Kingdom. "He grew an exceeding great man, swelling with titles," says Strype. After enumerating these— about a dozen in all—the historian adds, "Because he was thus great, so he also was a very generous and good man, and a sincere favourer of the Gospel; he was entirely beloved by those that professed it, and for the most part by the populacy; and, therefore, was commonly called *The Good Duke.*" Others judging him from a different standpoint, speak of him in far less flattering terms. It must, however, be admitted that in his exalted position he displayed high ability, and did much to favour the great work of the Reformation. Nevertheless his government was marred by such great faults that Warwick, Earl of Northumberland, his rival and enemy, found it easy to head a powerful party against him in 1549. A marriage between his daughter and Warwick's son stilled the opposition for a brief season: but Warwick's ambition and hatred did not long rest. On 16th October, 1551, the Duke was suddenly arrested on a charge of conspiracy and high treason, and committed to the Tower. His trial took place on 1st of December, when he was found guilty of felony and con- demned to death. He was executed on Tower Hill, January 22, 1552, and met his doom with great calmness. While he was repeating, for the third time, the name of Jesus, the executioner with one stroke of the axe severed his head from his body.

Less than three years before, many of the witnesses of this tragic sight had seen another execution on the same spot, and, probably, by the same headsman. It was that of the Duke's own brother,

THOMAS, LORD SEYMOUR OF SUDELEY,

and Lord High Admiral, of whose condemnation and death he had been the chief cause. The brothers lived for some years on good terms, and it was by the Duke's influence Sir Thomas was raised to the peerage, and put into possession not only of the lordship of Sudeley, in Gloucestershire, but of other estates in no fewer than eighteen counties! Bold, ambitious, and unprincipled, Lord Seymour aimed at yet higher rank and greater wealth. Almost immediately after the death of Henry VIII., he sought and easily won the hand of the Queen Dowager, Catherine Parr. This unfortunate lady, whom he treated with great indignity, died at Sudeley Castle, in September, 1548, a few days after having given birth to a daughter. His proud and reckless spirit repeatedly brought him into difficulties, till at length he was sent to the Tower in January, 1549. Proceedings were taken against him on the confession of Sir William Sharington, master of the Mint at Bristol. Sir William, who was charged with clipping, coining base money, and other frauds, confessed his guilt, and implicated Baron Seymour, whose trial, such as it was, a flagrantly unjust proceeding, resulted in his condemnation, and he was beheaded on March 20, 1549.

The rich rectory of *Pewsey* was held for more than half a century by the Rev.

JOSEPH TOWNSHEND,

who was instituted in 1764, and died in 1816. He was of Clare Hall, Cambridge ; and in early life was for a short time associated with Calvinistic Methodism, occasionally officiating in Lady Huntingdon's Chapel at Bath. His mind was active, and works on various subjects proceeded from his pen. *Free Thoughts on Despotic and Free Governments* was published in 1781 : and the following year *Dissertations on the Poor Laws*. In 1786 he visited the Continent, and then wrote his *Journey through Spain*. Having in early life studied medicine, he published *The Physician's Vade Mecum;* and shortly afterwards *A Guide to Health*, designed specially for the use of students. These political and scientific works were followed by a book of sermons ; and by a last work in two quarto volumes on *The Character of Moses*. In this latter production Townshend displays great knowledge as a linguist.

As a county magistrate Mr. Townshend interested himself much in the roads being well kept, and being a man of great stature, his friends sometimes called him " The Colossus of Roads."

WILLIAM COLLINGBOURNE,

a gentleman living in the reign of Richard III., took some measures of opposition against that unpopular King and his chief ministers. Among other means he used the pen, and wrote satirical rhymes which he posted for the edification of his neighbours upon the church doors. The lines which gave highest offence formed the now well-known couplet :—

> "The Cat, the Rat, and Lovel the Dogge,
> Rule all England under a Hogge."

Whatever wit was required for the composition of this enigma, little was needed to solve it. Sir William Catesby, Sir Richard Ratcliffe, and Lord Lovell were the ministers of a King whose crest was a boar. Collingbourne was indicted for sedition, and being found guilty was executed. In his indictment he is styled of Lydiard, in Wiltshire, but he is generally thought to have been a native of *Collingbourne Kingston* or *Collingbourne Ducis*.

Collingbourne Kingston reminds us again of

JOHN NORRIS,

whom we have already noticed at Bemerton. Here he was born at the parsonage in 1657. He went to Exeter College, Oxford, and in 1680 was chosen a fellow of All Souls. After being rector of Newton St. Loe, Somersetshire, he became rector of Bemerton, where he died a martyr to intense study, 1711, aged 54. "Mild, humble, and amiable in his manners," says one writer, "he was an enthusiast as a man, a mystic in theology, and in philosophy an idealist. He attacked Locke's Essay on the *Human Understanding*, and wrote against Dodwell on the *Immortality of the Soul*. His works are chiefly on moral and theological subjects, and against the Quakers, Calvinists, and other seceders of the day, and his sermons are written in a clear, pleasing, and pathetic style. He wrote also some poems."

Henry Scudder, B.D., of Cambridge University, who was minister of Collingbourne Ducis during the Commonwealth, was a strong presbyterian. He was the author of a popular work, *The Christian's Daily Walk*, and died before the Restoration.

JEREMY CORDEROY,

a divine of some note in the seventeenth century, was a native of *Chute*.

L

He was an Oxford Student, and became one of the chaplains of Merton. For some reason he refused to accept any living, but devoted much of his time to writing works of divinity. In opposition, probably, to some of the extreme doctrines of the time, he insists with great warmth on the necessity of moral rectitude in order to the attainment of salvation.

North Tidworth is noted as the birthplace of

ROBERT MATON,

a celebrated divine, who was born about 1607. He was educated at Wadham College, Oxford, and obtained a benefice somewhere in his native country. He wrote several works of a prophetical character, one being *A Discourse on Gog and Magog*. The novelty of his opinions excited much attention, and awakened both admiration and opposition. Another of his books, probably his last, entitled *The Fifth Monarchy, &c.*, was published in 1655.

In the beginning of this century the manor house of Tidworth was the property of a gentleman named Edward Poore, a person of most singular character. Having travelled for some years in Italy he retired to Tidworth, where he lived in seclusion, and affected the manners and customs of the Italians. In music and literature he found abundant amusement, and left behind him piles of manuscripts, on a variety of subjects.

Reminiscences of

THOMAS ASSHETON SMITH,

by Sir John Eardley Wilmot, Bart., is an interesting memoir of a gentleman of fox-hunting celebrity, who for more than thirty years resided in that part of *South Tidworth* which is in Wiltshire. Mr. Smith was a man of great wealth, and of much originality and force of character. Many anecdotes are told of his extreme liberality. He died in 1858.

The families of country clergymen have given to England many of her best sons. Men eminent in religion and learning, science and art, politics and arms, have been born in the rural parsonage. Some instances of this have already come under our notice ; in

JOSEPH ADDISON

we have another. His father, Launcelot Addison, was rector of the parish of *Milston*, where the eminent essayist was born in 1672. Of his early life we have little knowledge. One instance, however, of his sensitive character as a child is recorded. While at school, somewhere in the neighbourhood of his home, he one day committed some fault. Painfully apprehensive of disgrace or punishment, he escaped to the fields, where, feeding on fruits and lodging in a hollow tree, he remained some time in concealment before he was discovered by his friends. At the age of fifteen he was entered at Queen's College, Oxford, where he obtained an intimate acquaintance with classical literature, and distinguished himself by several elegant Latin compositions. One of these, on the accession of William and Mary to the throne, secured his election into Magdalen College, on the founder's bene-faction. Through the patronage and influence of Lord Somers and others, he obtained a pension of £300 a year to enable him to travel, and he accordingly spent some time abroad. This allowance was discontinued on the death of William, but Addison received some good appointments, and continued to prosecute various literary labours. He became a large contri-butor to the *Tatler* and the *Spectator*, and subsequently to the *Guardian*. He also composed the tragedy of *Cato*, and produced some other poetical pieces.

Addison sat for Malmsbury in the House of Commons which was elected in 1708 ; but did not attain any distinction in his parliamentary career. He was a silent member. He once rose to speak, but, unable to overcome his diffidence, had to resume his seat with his speech undelivered.

By his marriage, in 1716, with the Dowager Countess of Warwick, whom he had found it hard to win, he did not gain a prize. Her haughty temper neither contributed to his domestic comfort, nor beneficially influenced his habits. His matrimonial career of three years " formed an experience through which he would not have lived again for the wealth of the kingdom of Morocco. He was the most miserable husband that was ever burdened with a middle-aged shrew, who had no respect for him, and for whom he had no love." A year or two after his marriage he resigned his public offices and retired on a handsome pension. But he did not cease to work. His *Evidences of Christianity* was written at this time. He died at Holland House, Kensington, June 17, 1719.

The life and character, as well as the abilities and writings, of Addison have been freely discussed. Both among his contemporaries and by posterity widely different opinions have been formed of the man and his works. While some pronounce the most unfavourable verdicts, others express the highest admiration. Referring to "his image skilfully graven," in Poets' Corner, Westminster Abbey, Macaulay says : " Such a mark of national respect was due to the unsullied statesman, to the accomplished scholar, to the master of pure English eloquence, to the consummate painter of life and manners."

The little parish of *Boscombe*, in the valley of the winter-flowing Bourn, reminds us of

RICHARD HOOKER,

to whom Locke's epithet, "the judicious," attaches as closely as his own proper baptismal name. When Master of the Temple, he petitioned the Archbishop of Canterbury for removal. Controversy was prevailing, and Hooker wrote, "I am weary of the noise and oppositions of this place," He sighed for some rural parsonage, where in quietness he could pursue his studies, and carry on and complete without interruption, a line of argument he had projected. He was therefore made rector of Boscombe, in 1591, and was also, as a step to further preferment, appointed to a minor prebend at Salisbury. In this retired parish, with its few score of inhabitants, he found the tranquillity he sought, and during his residence of four years produced and published *Four Books of the Laws of Ecclesiastical Polity*. Hooker left Boscombe in 1595, for the rectory of Bishopsbourne, near Canterbury, where he died in 1600.

The small village of *Idmiston*, also in the vale of the Winterbourne, was for some years the residence of the Rev.

JOHN BOWLE,

an eccentric clergyman, commonly called *Don Bowle*, from his attachment to the Spanish language. He was descended from a Bishop of Rochester, and was educated at Oriel College, Oxford. His erudition embraced antiquities, the classics and most modern languages of Europe. He published a splendid edition of *Don Quixote*, edited *Miscellaneous Pieces of Ancient English Poesie*, and contributed a variety of articles to the *Gentleman's Magazine*. Dr. Douglas, Bishop of Salisbury, who did much to expose William Lauder's forgeries on Milton, says Bowle was the first to detect that unprincipled writer. He died on his birthday, Oct. 26, 1788, aged 68. A distinguished member of an eminent Wiltshire family,

HENRY RICHARD FOX, LORD HOLLAND,

was born at *Winterslow*, in 1773. Early in life he gave proofs of great talents, and manifested a special interest in political subjects. In this branch of his education he was favoured with the instructions of his paternal uncle, the celebrated Charles James Fox. When he appeared in public life he soon became a prominent figure. In parliament, he was especially famed for his skill as a debater. For many years he took a most active part in national affairs, and his residence, Holland House, Kensington, where he and Lady Holland exercised princely hospitality, was long known as the resort of the most distinguished men of the time. He died at this famed residence, Oct. 22, 1840.

SIR BENJAMIN COLLINS BRODIE, BART.,

whose name is eminent in the annals of medical science, was also a native of Winterslow, of which parish his father was rector. He was born in 1783, and received his early education chiefly from his father. His professional studies were carried on in London under Mr. Abernethy and Dr, (afterwards) Sir Alexander Crichton; and, as a pupil of Sir Edward Home. at St. George's Hospital. Of this Hospital he was elected assistant surgeon in 1808, and subsequently surgeon. In 1810, in consequence of a contribution to the "Philosophical Transactions," he was chosen a fellow of the Royal Society. His reputation steadily grew; in 1832 he was appointed Sergeant Surgeon to Queen Adelaide; and two years afterwards was created a Baronet. The University of Oxford honoured him with the degree of D.C.L. in 1850; and in 1858 he became president of the Royal Society. His practice was extensive and his professional writings numerous. He died Oct. 19, 1865, leaving an interesting "Autobiography," which was published in 1865, with his works, in three volumes, edited by Charles Hawkins, F.R.C.S.

An oft-told Winterslow tale must not be omitted. On a dark October night in 1816, as the Exeter mail drove up to the Pheasant Inn, or Winterslow Hut, a lioness which had escaped from a travelling menagerie attacked one of the horses. A mastiff boldly came to the rescue, but was immediately killed by the savage beast, which was at last, with great difficulty, secured by its keeper.

The Fox family originally belonged to the straggling village of *Farley*, where

SIR STEPHEN FOX,

the first of the name who became conspicuous in public life, was born 27 March, 1627. Having in the civil war espoused the royal cause, he was appointed to important offices by Charles II., by whom he was knighted in 1665, and made a lord commissioner of the Treasury in 1679. He retired from public life in 1701, but had the honour of being selected by Queen Anne to conduct her when going in procession to her coronation, April 23, 1702.

Sir Stephen served in several parliaments for Salisbury and Westminster. His charities were large and numerous. Chelsea Hospital was first projected by him, and he contributed £13,000 to assist in its institution. He built a church and an almshouse in his native village and several churches in other parts of the kingdom.

His son Stephen became Earl of Ilchester, and his son Henry, Baron Holland. His grandson, the Right Hon. Charles James Fox, to whose memory there is a marble tablet in Farley Church, will ever rank among the most illustrious of British statesmen.

Brickworth, in *Whiteparish*, was the birthplace of

WILLIAM EYRE,

a nonconformist minister of some note. He was educated at Magdalen Hall, Oxford, and became rector of St. Edmund's, Salisbury. His doctrinal opinions, which were highly Calvinistic, brought him into controversy with Baxter, Eedes and others. Being ejected in 1662 he retired to an estate of his own at Melksham, where he died in January, 1670.

DR. RALEIGH,

eldest son of Sir Carew, and grandson of Sir Walter Raleigh, was a native of the little town of *Downton*. He was a student of Magdalen College, Oxford, and became Chaplain to Charles I. and dean of Wells. In common with many other clergymen on both sides, he suffered greatly during the war, and was at length kept in custody in his own house at Wells, where he was at last murdered by a shoemaker, to whose tender mercies he had been committed. This inhuman wretch, who treated him with great cruelty, is said to have stabbed him because he refused to show him a letter he had written to his wife.

Trafalgar House in the parish of *Standlinch*, six miles south of Salisbury, reminds us of another great English name, the illustrious Lord Nelson, for whose heirs this fine estate was purchased by Act of Parliament in 1814, and is now held by the Right Hon. Earl Nelson.

Clarendon Park, in the parish of *Alderbury*, is a place of great historical interest. The royal palace, which formerly stood within its bounds, was a favourite resort of some of the early English Kings. It is specially remarkable for the Parliament which Henry II. assembled here in 1164, and by which the celebrated "Constitutions of Clarendon" were enacted. By these laws, Blackstone says, "The King checked the power of the Pope and Clergy; and greatly narrowed the total exemption they claimed from the secular jurisdiction." The murder of Thomas à Becket was the result of his opposition to these enactments. It is remarkable that Becket was at one time connected with this neighbourhood. Aubrey says "In the common field of Winterbourn is the celebrated path called St. Thomas Becket's path. It leads from the village up to Clarendon Park. St. Thomas Becket, they say, was sometime a curé priest at Winterbourn, and did use to go along this path up to a Chapell in Clarendon Parke, to say masse, and very likely 'tis true."

A descendant of the family of Bouverie, which in 1568 had been driven from Flanders to England by religious persecution, purchased the *Longford* estate in 1730. He became Lord Longford, and was succeeded by his eldest son Pleydell, who had been created Earl of Radnor, and whose eldest son, Jacob, became second Earl in 1776. He was appointed Recorder of Salisbury, and erected the Council House in that city. He died in 1828, and was succeeded by his eldest son the Right Hon.

WILLIAM PLEYDELL BOUVERIE, THIRD EARL OF RADNOR,

whose long, close, and honourable connection with Wiltshire entitles him to notice.

As Viscount Folkestone he was elected for the borough of Downton in 1801, and the next year was returned for Salisbury. This latter seat he retained till he succeeded to the Earldom. On his father's death he became Recorder of the city. Earl Radnor, both as a commoner and a peer, pursued a strongly marked liberal course. He was a politician greatly in advance of the majority of his own rank. The Abolition of Slavery, Roman Catholic Emancipation, the great Reform Bill, and the Repeal of the Corn Laws, all received his earnest support. He boldly expressed his sympathy with many of the views of Cobbett, whom he helped to enter parliament. "For some years after his accession to the title," says one writer, "Lord Radnor may be said to have been the most perfect specimen of a real Radical in the Upper House." "Some twenty or thirty years ago," said the "*Times*," in 1869, "when he was in full health and strength, his handsome figure and honest and pleasant face were familiar enough to his brother peers, who were often amused at the strong denunciations hurled at him by such men as Earl Roden and the Earl of Winchelsea, on account of his bitter invectives against what he considered the corruptions of the Established Church, and the exclusion of Dissenters from the Universities."

When in later years Earl Radnor took up his residence at Coleshill, in Berkshire, and turned his attention to agriculture and horticulture, he did so with much success, and soon became famous for his shorthorn cattle, Southdown sheep, and white pigs.

As a landlord and a neighbour, and in all the relations of life, the Earl was highly esteemed for his integrity, Christian benevolence, and great generosity. His death occurred April 9, 1869, within a few days of his ninetieth birthday. He was laid to rest in the family mausoleum at Britford Church.

OBSERVANT readers must have noted the great age which many of the subjects of our biographical sketches attained. In Bailey's *Records of Longevity*, published in 1857, we find notes of thirty-one Wiltshire Centenarians. Of these, eight belonged to Salisbury—namely, Mrs. Scott, widow, a lacemaker, who died 1750, aged 105: Mark Street, a saddler, who died the same year, aged 101: Francis Atkins, porter at the palace gate from the time of Bishop Burnet to the period of his death, 1761, at the age of 104 : Mrs. Sholmine, widow, who reached 103 years and died 1771 : Mrs. Bacon, died 1779, aged 100 ; Mrs. Poer, widow, entered her 102nd year, and died 1791 : Matthew Merris, inmate of an almshouse, died in 1799 at the age of 100 ; and Ann Fulford, who died about the same period at the same age.

The parish register at Bremhill contains the following remarkable entry :—1696. Buried Sept. 29. Edith Goldie, Grace Young, and Elizabeth Wiltshire ; their united ages make 300 years." James Grist, farmer, died at Bulford, 1760, aged 108. Mrs. Port, widow, who died at Great Cheverell the following year, was 105. The Rev. Mr. Crook, of Brinkworth, died in 1763, at the age of 100 : and Jane Owen, widow, died at Cricklade the same year, one year his senior. Jane Talbot died at Oaksey 1765, aged 105. At Warminster Mr. Cockey died in 1767, at the age of 100 ; and in the same town in 1813, Betty Crook, who had been a domestic servant in one family for 90 years, closed her life at the age of 105. John Haynes, of Wootton Bassett, died at the same age in 1767. An agricultural labourer, Thomas Pearce, died at Hawly Hill Farm in 1772, aged 112. With the parish of Stratford-sub-Castle the names of three centenarians are associated : Mrs. Bremdon died 1779, aged 103 ; Roger Warne died 1785, and Mrs. Blake died 1791, each aged 100. George Phillips died at Stourhead in 1780, aged 106 ; and in 1782 John Isles died at Bradford-on-Avon, aged 103. Ann Simms, already noticed, died at Studley Green in 1785, at the extraordinarily great age of 113. John Saunders, of Old Sarum, lived to be 106, and died 1799. Mrs. Cross, widow, who died at Staverton in 1802, was born in 1700. At Tisbury, Robert Oberne died in 1810, aged 101 ; and at Sevenhampton, Mary Davis, widow, died in 1813, aged 103. The Rev. Mr. Bedwell, who held the rectory of Odstock for 73 years, lived to 103, and died in 1814. To this long list may be added the name of Thomas Fisher, a native of Oaksey, who died at Sapperton, Gloucestershire, Oct. 11, 1869, aged, at least, 105 years. The annals of the county would doubtless furnish many other instances.

CONCLUSION.

"Mark thou them who well and wisely
Lived and loved and wrought of yore;
If thou heed them well and wisely,
Thou of them shalt learn good lore;
Learn to live as well and wisely
As they lived, or even more."

"Ovum tempus habemus, operemur bonum."
Inscription on Pillar, Kelloway's Bridge.

"Life steals away,—this hour, oh man, is lent thee
Patient to work the work of Him that sent thee."
Paraphrase by W. L. BOWLES.

UR journeyings have again brought us to Salisbury, where our projected tour ends, and we here offer, by way of conclusion, a few general facts and observations.

A cathedral city, with its ecclesiastical buildings and institutions, naturally suggests inquiry as to the religious history of the district of which for hundreds of years it has been the centre. Such inquiry in the case of Wiltshire would result in a large amount of interesting information. From an early period some form of Christianity has exercised its influence among the inhabitants of these parts. Almost side by side Druid priests served at altars "wet with human gore," and meek messengers from distant lands lifted up the standard of the cross. Early in the tenth century Plegmund Archbishop of Canterbury established a separate diocese in this county. As time went on churches and religious institutions grew and multiplied, and priests and monks abounded. Bishop Tanner gives a list of more than sixty Monasteries and other religious houses. To what extent their influence was for good we cannot now decide: but in Wiltshire, as elsewhere, the Church was marred by evils within herself, and assailed by opponents from without. The power of Wickliffe's teaching was felt, and two, at least, of his Wiltshire followers suffered death. Fuller relates that about 1503 Richard Smart was burnt at Salisbury for reading a book called "Wicliff's Wicket" to one Thomas Stillman, who was afterwards burnt in Smithfield.

The Reformation had many friends in the county, three of whom, if not more, were added to "the noble army of martyrs" in Queen Mary's reign. Their names and vocations are given by Fuller: "John Spicer, Free Mason; William Coberly, Taylor; John Maundrell, Husbandman." These men, who were all residents of Keevil, were burnt at Fisherton, in April, 1556. Coberley was a Gloucestershire man, a native of Coberley, near Cheltenham. Two husbandmen, John Hunt and Richard White, of Marlborough, who were persecuted at Salisbury, in 1558, honourably rank as "Confessors" in Fuller's list.

The Puritanism of the Stuart period had its representatives in many a Wiltshire parish. So widely had its principles spread, and so deeply rooted had they become, that Bartholomew Day in 1662 found no fewer than 56 of the clergy ready to suffer ejection from their livings rather than comply with the Act of Uniformity. Among these were several men of eminence, including Dr. John Harding, a successor of Crisp, at Brinkworth; Thomas Rosewell, M.A., of Sutton Mandeville; Dr. Humphrey Chambers, of Pewsey; and Peter Ince, of Donhead. Eight others (including a "John Norris," probably the father of the one we have noticed) were also ejected, but afterwards conformed. Some of the Congregational churches now existing in the county date their origin from this period, and many curious and interesting facts may be found in their early records. This denomination has greatly increased, and is now a large and influential community.

There are few religious bodies of which the historical records are so full and accurate as those of the Society of Friends. The voluminous journal of its great founder, George Fox, abounds with accounts not only descriptive of his own labours and sufferings, but throwing much light upon the times. His work in Wiltshire was abundant, and his success, especially in some parts, encouraging. Numerous meetings were originated, the usual persecution being incurred and patiently endured. Besse's work on the

Sufferings of Friends supplies sad evidence of the cruel treatment which Wiltshire Quakers, in common with others, experienced from magistrate and mob. Aubrey shared the common prejudice against them. Writing of Corston he says, "In the Church nothing to be found ; the modern zeal has been reforming hereabout. Surely this tract of land, Gloucestershire and Somersetshire, encline people to zeal. Heretofore nothing but Religious Houses, now nothing but Quakers and Fanatiques."

In spite of all, the work went on and prospered. Oliver Sansom, a Berkshire Friend, who died in 1710, often visited this county in the exercise of a ministry which, judging from his character, must have been singularly tender and persuasive. In his earlier days he was probably a fellow worker with Fox. At intervals from 1716 to 1731, Thomas Story, an eminent minister of this society, travelled to Salisbury and most of the chief towns, holding meetings which he generally speaks of as "large, peaceable, and satisfactory," though others are described as " small, heavy, and drowsy." While here, as elsewhere, there has been a growth of Friends' principles there has been a decrease in the number of their members.

"John Wesley in Wiltshire" might form the subject of a little volume. His own remarkable journal would supply numerous facts illustrative of the religious condition of the county during the period of his labours. His first mention of Wiltshire occurs under date Feb. 27th, 1738, when he writes, " I took coach for Salisbury, and had several opportunities of conversing seriously with my fellow travellers." Subsequent records mention frequent preaching visits to Salisbury, Devizes, Bradford, Trowbridge, Chippenham, Marlborough, Westbury, and other towns, besides villages and hamlets. Two or three extracts may afford glimpses not only of the times, but of the man and his work :—July 17th, 1739. He called on a gentleman at Bradford, who had on one occasion before shown him some favour, but who now not only received him coldly, but, says Wesley, "told me plainly one of our own College had informed him they always took me to be a little crack-brained at Oxford."

January 13, 1749, "At the Devises : the town was in an uproar from end to end as if the French were just entering."

Oct. 17, 1753. "I began visiting the societies in Wiltshire, and found much cause to praise God on their behalf."

Oct. 2, 1754. "I walked to Old Sarum, which in spite of common sense, without house or inhabitant, still sends two members to Parliament."*

Oct. 2, 1764. "I breakfasted at the Devises with Mr. B——, a black swan, an honest lawyer!"

Oct, 5, 1768. "I rode over to Maiden Bradley, and preached at a little distance from the town, to as serious a congregation as I ever saw, many of whom were in tears. It is a wonder there should be room for the Gospel here, among so many Lords and gentlemen. But indeed they neither meddle nor make; and this is all we desire of them."

Recording his preaching at Bradford, Oct. 20, 1769, he says with some little warmth of indignation, "The beasts of the people were tolerably quiet till I had nearly finished my sermon. They then lifted up their voice, especially one, called a gentleman, who had filled his pocket with rotten eggs: but," he adds with quiet humour and evident enjoyment of the fun, "a young man coming unawares, clapped his hands on each side, and smashed them all at once. In an instant there was perfume all over, though it was not so sweet as balsam."

In some of his later visits to Sarum he refers to a Captain Webb, one of his preachers, in a way which seems to connect him with that locality. This gentleman, whom he elsewhere describes as being "all life and fire," made a most unfavourable impression upon Jay who met him when dining with Wesley at Lady Maxwell's. Speaking of those present he says:— "There was a Capt. Webb, deprived of one eye at the battle of Bunker's Hill, who held forth commonly without doors, in regimentals. As I wished to hear Mr. Wesley talk nothing could be more mortifying than the incessant garrulity of this fanatical rodomontader; and I much wondered Mr. Wesley, who had such influence over his adherents, did not repress, or at least rebuke, some of his spiritual vagaries and supernatural exploits."

Wesley's last Wiltshire record is on Sept. 27, 1790, less than a month

* Wilts was at this time returning 34 representatives to Parliament, while the neighbouring County of Gloucester sent eight only.

before the close of his journal, and but little more than five months before his death, so that he was in the eighty-eighth year of his age and the sixty-fifth of his ministry, when he wrote under this date :—"Monday I left Bristol, about eleven. I preached in the Devises, and in the evening at Sarum. I do not know that ever I saw the house so crowded before, with high and low, rich and poor; so I hope we shall again see fruit here also."

Wiltshire was the scene of many of Whitefield's evangelizing labours, in which he had some hearty fellow workers. The opposition that arose was unusually strong and bitter. Referring to the persecutions through which the great preacher and his friends had to pass about 1742, one of his biographers—J. P. Gledstone—writes :—"Wiltshire had for some time been in commotion through the animosity of several clergymen, and White-field felt himself obliged to put the facts before the Bishop of Sarum [Dr. Sherlock], who, however, does not seem to have interfered to stop the disgraceful proceedings. Churchwardens and overseers were strictly forbidden to let the Methodists have anything out of the parish; they obeyed the clergy, and told the poor they would famish them, if in no other way they could stop them from joining the new sect. Most of the poor, some of them with large families, braved the threat, and suffered for their constancy the loss of goods and friends. A few denied that they had ever been to meetings; and some promised that they would go no more." These cruel measures probably promoted the progress of the movement : societies were formed and preachers were multiplied. Among others in after years, Rowland Hill followed in Whitefield's wake and preached in various parts of the county. His efforts though often met by opposition were nevertheless attended by much success. One remarkable instance is given by Mr. Charlesworth in his *Life of Rowland Hill*. This eccentric but excellent man was once preaching in the open air at Devizes, when one of his opponents adopted a mode of annoyance worthy the malignant ingenuity of a fiend. Filling his pocket with snakes he got near the preacher, and watching his opportunity he threw three at once upon him. One of the reptiles coiled round his arm and another fastened on his neck. "Perceiving," said Mr. Hill, "that they were harmless, I merely took them off and threw them behind me away from the crowd; some of the people immediately drove away the sinner, and the result was increased attention and several conversions to God. Soon after the rebel came again to hear me ; and he that would have alarmed me by serpents was himself rescued from the old serpent, and became for many years a steadfast follower of the Lamb of God."

Baptists appeared in Wiltshire during the seventeenth century, and various branches of the denomination, holding a diversity of theological opinions, have spread through the county. Their chapels and preaching stations are numerous, being found not only in the larger towns, but in many of the villages also.

The Primitive Methodists, preaching the same doctrines and animated by the same zeal as their earlier brethren, have long laboured in various parts of the county with much success, and are now a numerous body.

The See of Salisbury has been held by some distinguished prelates, whose names are not the least among English Bishops. Of these, Dr. John Jewell, who was consecrated in 1560, and died in 1571, was one of the most eminent. Dr. Gilbert Burnet, who filled the episcopal chair from 1689 till 1715, was a learned and benevolent man, an historian as well as a divine. Dr. Benjamin Hoadley, who held the diocese from 1723 till his removal to Winchester in 1735, was one of the most polemical writers of his time. He was almost constantly engaged in controversy, and whatever may be thought of his opinions, it must be admitted that he conducted his arguments with great force and ingenuity. The magnificent monument recently erected in the Cathedral to the memory of the late Bishop Hamilton is one, among many proofs, of the high esteem in which that prelate was held.

Jay quotes Dr. Johnson as saying "there is hardly a life of which some useful narrative may not be furnished." "Yes ;" he himself adds, "there are many who never see a college, nor enter a pulpit, nor publish a book, who serve their generation by the will of God. They embody and fulfil religion in their private stations ; and though they make no figure in the annals of worldly renown, are great in the sight of the Lord."

In closing these Notes we cannot but remark that in our researches we have met with scores of names in all classes, with which high moral excellence, or superior talents or usefulness of life has been associated, but which our space would not permit us to particularly notice. As instances we may refer to two biographical sketches by the writer of these Notes. One, *The Art Student*, being a brief account of Albert Gibbons, a native of *Oaksey*, a young artist of great promise, who was drowned in the Serpentine, Hyde Park, July 17, 1868, at the age of 23 ; the other, *An Old Disciple*, a short narrative of the useful Christian life of William Wilkins, a native of *Ashton Keynes*, and for fifty years a blacksmith at Siddington, who died at Cirencester, Feb. 12, 1873, in his 84th year.

But, who shall tell how many good men and true have served their generation, and passed away altogether unrecorded ? In every town and hamlet of this county, as well as of every other, such characters have appeared and such lives have been lived. Worth and talent are not confined to any period, place, or class. God is no respecter of persons. His gifts are dispensed to high and low. Noble and peasant may receive of His grace and live to His glory. While He may be served in the mansion or the church, He may be as acceptably served in the smith's shop or at the weaver's loom, in the quarry or at the plough. Well and beautifully has the poet of Bemerton sung :—

> " All may of Thee partake :
>   Nothing can be so mean,
> Which with his tincture (for thy sake)
>   Will not grow bright and clean.
>
> A servant with this clause
>   Makes drudgery divine :
> Who sweeps a room, as for Thy laws,
>   Makes that and th' action fine."

www.ingramcontent.com/pod-product-compliance
Lightning Source LLC
Chambersburg PA
CBHW031110020726

47495CB00007B/2142

9783337373924